Ready -to- Reproduce Handouts

by Maryann Hudgins, M.Ed., LPCS &
Angela Tackett, M.Ed., LPCI

youth light inc.

© 2007
YouthLight, Inc.
Chapin, SC 29036

Cover Design by Amy Rule
Layout / Graphics by Amy Rule
Project Editing by Susan Bowman

ISBN

Library of Congress Number

10 9 8 7 6 5 4 3 2 1
Printed in the United States

About the Author

Maryann Hudgins, M.Ed., LPCS is a school counselor for the Grand Prairie Independent School District in Texas. She holds a bachelor's degree in Education from Bowling Green State University and a Master's degree from University of North Texas. She obtained her professional counselor's license in 1982. Mrs. Hudgins has worked in the elementary schools for over thirty years, and continues to work as the district's Lead Elementary Counselor and still serves as a campus counselor as well. Maryann is the mother of one fantastic son, J. P. and the proud wife of her husband, James, for the past twenty-five years.

Acknowledgements

I am so blessed to have had the best of the best Campus and Central Administrators over the years. It is for them that I felt the need to assist with this book of quick and easy topics to present during faculty meetings. They have always strived to do the most for each student and teacher when our time is at such a premium. I also would like to thank the creative and talented counselors that I have worked with over the years... some have retired and others are beginning... but each has taught me a trick or two along the way!

Dedication

I dedicate this book to my friends and colleagues in the Grand Prairie Independent School District who have made a second home for me and challenge me to always try to do my best! May we all see our children as Today's Pride and Tomorrow's Promise!

About the Author

Angela Tackett, M.Ed., is a school counselor for the Grand Prairie Independent School District in Texas. She holds a bachelor's degree in Social Work from University of Texas at Arlington and a Master's degree from Texas A & M - Commerce. She is a Licensed Social Worker and a certified special education teacher. Ms. Tackett has worked in the elementary schools for ten years as a social worker, special education teacher, and is now in her fourth year as a school counselor at Barbara Bush Elementary. She is presently working on her LPC and also plans to pursue her Registered Play Therapy certification in the near future.

Acknowledgements

I want to thank the staff and parents at Barbara Bush Elementary for their continued support over the years. I consider myself privileged to spend my days with your wonderful and caring children. The students teach me more than I could ever dream of teaching them. I am also blessed to have a group of counselors, especially my lead counselor and friend, Maryann Hudgins, that I can call at a moment's notice. Last, I would like to acknowledge and thank my incredible family for their love and support with everything that I pursue.

Dedication

I dedicate this book in memory of my best friend and biggest fan, my grandmother, Katherine Bible. Without her love, strength, guidance and support, getting to where I am today would have been a challenge and not near as fun! She is missed every minute of every day. I couldn't have asked for a better friend and role model.

Introduction

In order to make the best use of your time, this book offers a quick and easy way to bring valuable information to school staff members. Now if you need to fill in a short activity or distribute an informational handout on specific topics, this resource is right at your fingertips. This book includes a variety of topics and reproducible items to make presentations a breeze.

The collection included in the book offers the opportunity to share the information with teachers, parents, and students. Some days it is easier to address a problem with a quick handout whereas other times you are able to have a face to face meeting. You need to be prepared in all cases. Our hope is that you find these activities ready to share with those in need!

Best Wishes & Good Luck

- Maryann Hudgins, M.Ed., LPCS

- Angela Tackett, M.Ed., LPCI

 # Table of Contents

Table of Contents

 # Table of Contents

● ● ● ● ● ● ● ● ● ● ● ● ● ● ● ● ● ● ● ●

● ●

Table of Contents

Table of Contents

Chapter 1

CELEBRATING YOUR STAFF

What could feel better than to be the center of a celebration? This is not just for the kids anymore. When we are talking about school, the teachers need a boost, too! It is true that teachers are notorious for spending many of their own dollars on treats for deserving children. The tables are turned in this section of our book. We feel that even adults can enjoy a day or a week of special treatment. This comes in handy as a way to get to know each person's likes and dreams. It is also a time to acknowledge individuals for the hours of unpaid work they contribute to the children's education. Extra "pay" comes in the little things that we do for one another and the kind words we use as we recognize our peers.

Faculty Activities

Faculty Handouts

GET TO KNOW YOU BINGO!

Group members mingle and collect each other's names according to who matches each square. Fill in all of the squares for a game of blackout bingo or play four in a row, diagonal / vertical line, four corners, or set a timer.

Has a five letter name	The youngest sibling	Admits to being a die-hard fan of Wheel of Fortune	Has been snorkeling
_____	_____	_____	_____
Speaks *two* languages	Has a parent who works in education	Moved around more than 3 times growing up	Has *the* same number of siblings as you
_____	_____	_____	_____
Has sky-dived or bungee jumped	Was a girl / boy scout	Lived in *the* same house birth - 12th grade	Loves Mexican food
_____	_____	_____	_____
Has been in education for more than eight years	Admits to staying at school past 10pm	Is wearing yellow today	Has more than 4 brothers and sisters
_____	_____	_____	_____

DEVOTED STAFF COUPONS

STAFF PERSON OF THE WEEK	STAFF PERSON OF THE WEEK	STAFF PERSON OF THE WEEK
This coupon entitles you to one day off from one of your scheduled extra duties, ie. bus duty, cafeteria duty, etc. this week.	This coupon entitles you to your own parking spot in the front for the week.	This coupon entitles you to wear your jeans and school spirit shirt one extra day this week.
STAFF PERSON OF THE WEEK	STAFF PERSON OF THE WEEK	STAFF PERSON OF THE WEEK
This coupon entitles you to one free lunch from the cafeteria.	This coupon entitles you to one free ice cream from the cafeteria.	This coupon entitles you to 30 minutes of free time. The principal or assistant will come and sub for you!
STAFF PERSON OF THE WEEK	STAFF PERSON OF THE WEEK	STAFF PERSON OF THE WEEK
This coupon entitles you to one free "I Goofed" moment!!!	This coupon entitles you to leave school right after your kids are gone one day this week.	We appreciate you! Have a wonderful week!!!

DEVOTED STAFF PERSON OF THE WEEK

Each week a devoted staff member is recognized on a hallway bulletin board entitled, "Devoted Staff Person of the Week." Fill out this information sheet so that the students and parents can read these interesting facts to learn more about you. Also, bring special pictures of you and your family to add to the bulletin board display.

DEVOTED STAFF PERSON

MY FAMILY:	BIRTHDAY:	MY ADVICE TO STUDENTS:
	FAVORITE SCHOOL SUBJECT:	
	FAVORITE MOVIE OR TV SHOW:	
MY ROLE MODEL:	FAVORITE FOOD:	SAYING OR QUOTE I LIVE BY:
	FAVORITE PLACE TO SHOP:	
GROWING UP I ALWAYS WANTED TO...	FAVORITE SNACK:	SOMEDAY I WOULD LIKE TO...
	I LOVE TO...	

THINGS I LIKE...

This activity is very beneficial as a beginning of the year activity. Keep a file of these information sheets in a central location so that co-workers can refer to them when they want to treat others with their favorite item as a gesture of thanks or kindness.

Name: _____

List several of your favorite things in each category!

My Favorite Candy...	
My Favorite Pain Reliever Brand...	
My Favorite Fruit Types...	
My Favorite Crackers...	
My Favorite Chips...	
My Favorite Breath Mints & Gum...	
My Favorite Snacks...	
My Favorite Collectable Junk...	
My Favorite Lunch Foods...	
My Favorite Soft Drink...	
Other Items You Would Like To Tell Us About!	

Chapter 2

GETTING TO KNOW THE NEW STUDENT

When a new student arrives at your school for their first day it can be a bit overwhelming. The child may not know anyone and coming into a new school can be scary. Some schools have a Welcoming Committee made up of older students that show a new student around. If your school does not have a Welcoming Committee, you can choose two students to give him / her a tour. Along the way the student can be invited to redeem the coupons on the following pages at various places throughout the school. Following the coupons is a great tool to introduce the new student to some of the different faculty members and to learn what they do.

NEW STUDENT COUPONS

WELCOME NEW STUDENT

NEW STUDENT COUPON BOOK

THIS BOOK BELONGS TO:

_____

WELCOME NEW STUDENT

WELCOME TO OUR SCHOOL

We are very glad you are here! To help you become better acquainted, we would like you to turn in these coupons as you meet a few new faces.

WELCOME NEW STUDENT

TURN IN THIS COUPON TO YOUR TEACHER FOR...

one FREE homework pass.
(At teacher's discretion)

WELCOME NEW STUDENT

TURN IN THIS COUPON TO THE LIBRARIAN FOR...

a FREE bookmark and sticker.

WELCOME NEW STUDENT

TURN IN THIS COUPON TO THE SCHOOL NURSE FOR...

a FREE band-aid.

WELCOME NEW STUDENT

TURN IN THIS COUPON TO THE PRINCIPAL FOR...

a SURPRISE!

NEW STUDENT COUPONS

WELCOME NEW STUDENT

THIS COUPON IS GOOD FOR...

one FREE hug from:
A Teacher
The Principal
The Counselor

WELCOME NEW STUDENT

TURN IN THIS COUPON TO THE ASSISTANT PRINCIPAL FOR...

a FREE pencil

WELCOME NEW STUDENT

TURN IN THIS COUPON TO THE SCHOOL COUNSELOR TO...

play a game with two new friends.

WELCOME NEW STUDENT

TURN IN THIS COUPON TO THE CAFETERIA FOR...

a FREE ice cream treat during lunch.

WELCOME NEW STUDENT

TURN IN THIS COUPON TO THE SECRETARY FOR...

a FREE stamp.

WELCOME NEW STUDENT

We are so glad you are here! We are all here to help you!! Come and find us if you or your parents have any questions!!

ME AND MY SCHOOL COUNSELOR

My counselor, _____ is always here for me!
I can go and talk to her or him...
...when I need to talk.
...when my teacher suggests it.
...when my mom and dad want me to.
...when the principal asks me to.
...when the counselor invites me.

Sometimes the school counselor has a group of friends that she / he visits with for several weeks.

The school counselor also visits with every class in the school several times a year. This is called classroom guidance.

The school counselor might meet with my parents to discuss how I am doing.

I also can go and talk to her/him if I need to. All I have to do is write my name on the board outside the counselor's door and she/he will come and get me when she/he can. If it is an emergency, the teacher can have the office find the counselor for me.

The school counselor might talk with my teacher to see how things are going in class.

The school counselor is here for me!!! She / he wants to do everything possible for me to have a safe, happy and successful year!

ALL ABOUT THE NEW STUDENT

Purpose:

Here is an activity that you can do with your class when a new student arrives. This activity lets the new student share a little bit about himself / herself and also learn some things about the class.

Materials:

Paper and pencils

Procedures:

Have the students write down things that they would like to know about the new student. As they write down their question they are to think what their answer would be if they were asked the same question.

The new student also writes down some questions that he/ she might like to know about the school or people in the class.

Each person is given a chance to ask the new student their question and then in turn answer it as well.

This activity can last all day. Do a few in the morning and then some throughout the day. It is a good activity to do before or after recess and winding down at the end of the day. After everyone has had a chance the teacher can challenge the students by asking them if they remember what the answers were to some of the questions asked. For instance, "Does anyone remember what Susie's favorite sport is and why?"

TIPS FOR HELPING THE NEW STUDENT BECOME PART OF YOUR CLASSROOM'S FAMILY

1. Seat the new student near someone who can help him / her get acquainted with procedures and expectations and also serve as a role model for good behavior.

2. Be aware that most new students that come in are nervous and unsure of what to expect. These students may be very shy or extremely active. Make sure they are included in class discussions but remember to set up questioning for success. For instance, ask the student, "Is there anything you would like to add?" or "What are your thoughts on...?" Encourage the student to share and acknowledge the attempt, even if it is small.

3. Be up front with the student. Let him/ her know what the expectations are immediately so that there is no confusion in the future. Meeting with the parents as soon as possible is also recommended.

4. Have a student conference with the student early and talk about his / her experience at the other school. Assure the student that you are here to help and to listen whenever the student needs you. Building a relationship early on is vital, especially since you already have established relationships with the other students.

5. A mistake that some teachers make is after pairing up the new student with a peer helper, that helper is expected to always be in the group with the new student. Make sure the new student is able to get to know all of the students by encouraging him/ her to participate in group activities with various students in class.

6. *Remember:* The school counselor is here for the students if they need him / her. If the new student is apprehensive or upset that first day or so, the counselor can meet with him / her for reassurance.

Chapter 3

KEYS TO SUCCESSFUL LISTENING

The tools included in this chapter are varied and can be used with children, parents, teachers and other adults that want to be more effective in their communication skills. It is so important to break down the task of listening to very obvious and succinct steps. If one skill is mastered... listening would be the most important one for children and adults in today's world. We are so often concentrating on other things, that we miss the most important points of verbal messages. The following sheets might help to be reminders. The first is an activity that you can do with students or teachers to test their awareness. It is followed by parenting tips on listening and how to get more than a yes or no answer when asking your child questions. It takes practice to be able to consistently ask open ended questions.

SELF-AWARENESS

Name: _____ Date: _____

Shade the box to the right of each statement to measure your answer, like a thermometer!

	YES or Most of the Time	Sometimes or Not Sure	NO or Hardly Ever
1. I feel good about myself.			
2. I take part in group discussions.			
3. I know I am someone special.			
4. I know what put-ups / put-downs are and how they make people feel.			
5. I know how to express my anger without hurting myself or others.			
6. I know what peer pressure is.			
7. I know how to be a good friend.			
8. I cooperate with others.			
9. I am truthful and honest.			
10. I know what I need to work on: Here it is!			

Parents Listening to Kids

Tears, a laugh, a sullen face, a slammed door have meaning just as words do!

Let your child realize that you accept their feelings, whatever they may be, and therefore they can verbally express them to you if they choose to.

Let them know what you think they are feeling at a particular moment ... if you are wrong they will tell you!

Don't be caught up in the idea that you have to be "teaching" your child something all of the time. In doing this you may overlook their problem of the moment or a fun spontaneous conversation!

Make a conscious and obvious effort to understand and care about what your child is saying. They will appreciate being listened to.

The English language does not always follow its own rules. A child who is constantly corrected might have difficulty being spontaneous and sharing their experiences or feelings when they fear criticism.

Good communication patterns do begin early - but better communication is always possible!

Getting Kids to Listen

Be as quick, candid, and forthright as possible. You can communicate any number of messages and make your child feel that they are important and respected.

When your child asks a question, it is a sign that they are ready to listen and wants your opinion. Be careful to choose an appropriate time for discussing touchy subjects with your child.

It is always tempting to know all the answers. Sometimes we do know best. Sometimes we don't, and we are well advised not to pretend that we know it all. Admitting that we don't know is one way of conveying that we are not perfect, that we are human, too.

Sometimes parents worry that when they allow children to disagree with them they are undermining their respect and authority. Actually, children feel more respect for parents when they feel free to express their side of things. Permitting children to disagree with us shows them that we are strong enough to be challenged & big enough to back down if necessary!

Let them know that you can accept his good feelings and the so-called "bad" feelings - and still think no less of them. Telling your child that they should feel differently or that they should not feel what they do feel won't encourage them to listen to you.

Humiliating a child is a quick and sometimes permanent way to get a child not to listen. None of us want to talk or listen to another person if we feel they might cut us down.

Best Practice in Questioning

The approach of using open-ended questions yields more information from the child. This technique allows the child to feel more accepted, give more complete information, and explore more effectively. The best open-ended questions are <u>what</u> and <u>how</u> questions.

Could you tell me what happened in class?

- This question asks permission and is probably the most common, but be prepared to have the student say, "No," or "I don't want to talk about it!"

The following questions are better for a direct response.

What happened in class today?

What happened while you were in class?

How did it happen in class?

How did you get into trouble in class?

What can you do to solve this problem?

What will you do differently in the future?

How to be a Good Listener

MAKE EYE CONTACT: Be sure to look the speaker in the face most of the time, especially look at their eyes. If you forget to make eye contact, the speaker may think you are bored, withdrawn, or simply not listening. Also be culturally sensitive: some individuals may be uncomfortable with too much direct eye contact.

BODY LANGUAGE & LISTENING POSITION: Sit or stand in a comfortable position with your body aimed in the general area where the speaker is. Try to be in a relaxed position. Face the speaker and make appropriate eye contact. Be aware of: placement of arms, leaning forward when necessary, head nodding, personal space, and smiling.

SUMMARIZING THE SPEAKER'S MESSAGE: In your own words repeat what someone has just said. Some common ways include:

What I hear you saying is…
In other words...
So basically how you felt was…
What happened was…
Sounds like you're feeling…

The speaker then has a chance to know you have understood what they have said. This also gives the speaker the opportuinty to try to make the message more clear if they don't think you really understood.

ASK QUESTIONS FOR UNDERSTANDING: If something the speaker says is unclear to you, ask them a question to get more information. You don't want to misunderstand or agree with something that was not clear to you. It is important to ask for something to be repeated rather than to just agree because you are afraid to offend the speaker.

MAKE COMMENTS, ANSWER QUESTIONS: When the speaker stops or pauses, you can be a good listener by making comments about the same subject. If you change the topic suddenly, they may think you weren't listening.

OPENNESS: Listen with openness. Be a supportive, but neutral listener. It is so important to keep opinions out of a conversation that needs to be non-judgmental. If you are there to help, be there with an open mind.

Chapter 4

EFFECTIVE COMMUNICATION

Learning to communicate effectively can dramatically increase the relationship that one has with others. Included in this chapter is an activity that will help students learn to actively listen to you, and each other, as well as help them problem-solve and identify their own feelings and the feelings of others. This chapter also includes a poster to remind students how to actively listen, tips for teachers when communicating with parents, and also ways to record comments to parents in a way that solicits positive communication.

ASKING OPEN QUESTIONS*

Purpose: This activity teaches students the most facilitative way to ask questions to show they are listening and that they care about what others say.

Materials: Paper and pencils

Procedures: Explain to the students that some ways of asking questions are clearly better than others. The most open questions usually begin with the words, "What" or "How." Though there are many other ways to construct questions, these are usually the most inviting.

Questions that begin with "Why" can arouse defenses because it may sound like you are making an accusation. For example, a better way to ask the question, "Why do you feel that way?" would be, "What happened that bothered you so much?"

The following are examples of open "What" and "How" questions:

- What is your favorite animal?
- How is that animal like you?
- What is your favorite thing about school?
- How would you change school, if you could?

Write the following questions on the board. Then have the students reword the questions using a more inviting "What" or "How" question.

1. "Why don't you like school?"

2. "Are you going to try something different?"

3. "Did you work things out with your friend?"

4. "Can you tell me about it?"

5. "Why do you feel that way?"

Follow-Up: Have one person tell a brief description of something that happened to him / her during this past week. When the story is finished, brainstorm several possible "What" and "How" questions that could be asked. Be sure that the questions follow the story and do not lead the person away from what was said. Remember, a good question follows the speaker's lead and demonstrates that you are interested in what he / she is saying.

* adapted from Bowman & Bowman (1997). *Meaningful Mentoring: A Handbook of Effective Strategies, Projects and Activities.* Chapin, SC: YouthLight, Inc.

SUMMARIZING AND REFLECTING FEELINGS

Purpose: This activity teaches students to be active listeners by practicing good listening skills.

Material: Timer

Procedures: Model examples of active listening and summarizing (see "How to be a Good Listener" on page 26).

Have the students get in groups of two to three and brainstorm subjects they can discuss in their groups such as:

- How they spent the weekend
- A time that they got really angry
- A time that they had to make a difficult decision
- A time that they were upset
- What they want to be when they grow up and why
- A person they admire

Write the suggestions on the board for the students to choose.

Next, have them practice open questions and summarizing. Within each group, have the students appoint a speaker, a listener, and an observer (if there is a third person). Set a timer for 2 minutes. The speaker will talk about the topic and the listener will summarize what they hear after he / she finishes speaking. The observer will make suggestions on how the listener can improve his / her listening skills as well as which skills he / she excelled at.

Rotate until everyone has a turn being the speaker, the listener and the observer (if applicable). After everyone has a turn, go around again or talk about the experience.

- Was it easy to listen actively?
- Did you feel heard?
- What did you like about how the person listened to you?

Share with the students that when they actively listen they may hear things that the person didn't make a point to say or they may pick up on facial expressions or body language. Incorporate feeling words such as: upset, confused, frustrated, angry, overwhelmed, proud, excited, and lonely. Write the words on the board and talk about their meanings. Have the students list other feeling words to use.

Follow-Up: Eventually you will hear the students talking to one another at recess or during the day reflecting feelings and summarizing without even knowing it! When you teach a lesson and you see someone that perhaps is not fully engaged ask that person, "What do you hear me asking of you?" Or, ask the class, "Who can tell me what I am saying?"

COMMUNICATING TO PARENTS

It is sometimes difficult communicating effectively with parents. We do not want to put the parent on the defensive or insult them. We want to elicit their help when it comes to their child. However, when a child is acting out and we have to email, send a note, or even speak in person to them, the words we choose to use are VITAL!!! Here are some examples:

INSTEAD OF: Other students do not like him.

TRY: He is having trouble making and keeping friends.

WRITTEN: He needs assistance in getting along with others.

INSTEAD OF: She acts like a baby and pouts all the time.

TRY: She is having trouble doing things on her own and I am hoping as the year goes on and she becomes more mature she will feel more independent.

WRITTEN: She needs to work on being more independent.

INSTEAD OF: He is lazy.

TRY: Are there things at home that motivate him that I might try at school? He is having trouble completing assignments and needs lots of supervision.

WRITTEN: He seems to need constant direction and attention to complete assignments.

INSTEAD OF: She frequently hits and hurts others.

TRY: I am concerned that she is having trouble keeping her hands to herself and often uses her hands and fists to express herself.

WRITTEN: She's extremely physical in a negative way when dealing with others.

INSTEAD OF: He talks too much and is too loud.

TRY: I am pleased that he is excited about school however we need to work on reminding him when to talk out and when he starts getting a little loud.

WRITTEN: He is having difficulty staying on task during work time.

INSTEAD OF: She is a bully and picks on others.

TRY: She is becoming a leader in my class. It is important however, that she do so in a positive way and learn to compromise.

WRITTEN: She is having trouble compromising with others.

IDEAS FOR WRITTEN COMMUNICATION ON STUDENT PAPERWORK AND REPORT CARD

INSTEAD OF:	TRY:
Has been caught cheating	Has difficulty following rules
Lazy	Is unmotivated at times
Is selfish	Has trouble in group situations
Is mean and rude	Needs guidance in respecting self and others
Acts like a baby / pouts	Lack of maturity keeps him from going forward both academically and socially
Is a follower	Feels secure only in group situations and needs to become more independent
Always late / absent	Needs to be respectful of the importance of being at school every day and on time
Loud	Needs to work on communicating more quietly
Fights, hits or destroys property	Needs guidance on how to handle his anger and frustration

BEING AN ACTIVE LISTENER

FACE THE
PERSON TALKING

DO NOT FOLD
YOUR ARMS

HAVE
EYE CONTACT

DO NOT
INTERRUPT

SHOW YOU
UNDERSTAND
BY NODDING

WAIT FOR A
PAUSE AND THEN
SUMMARIZE WHAT
YOU HAVE HEARD

Chapter 5

DAILY CLASSROOM SAYINGS

The following pages include 50 positive daily sayings. Share each daily saying after the morning announcements or use as a journal entry or discussion point. Each saying is thought-provoking and will be a great way to start the day. So often we don't know how the day began for many of our children. Did they get themselves up and out by themselves? Were they upset by home situations? These new thoughts might be a way to refocus on a better start! When you run out of these sayings, or every Friday, ask students to provide sayings from their research or homes. They will be proud to try to bring one that all the students find interesting!

Faculty Handout

Daily Sayings

Each day I am improving, growing, and learning.

To dream is to sprinkle seeds of hope in the world.

If I'm not making mistakes, I'm probably not learning very much.

I will take time to laugh and have some fun today.

Today I will be as nice to myself as I would be to my best friend.

When I greet people warmly, I let them know that they are welcomed and important.

I am even more amazing than I thought.

Today I will soar higher than a kite!

Today I will practice thinking big by starting my own life goals list.

I will look for the positive things in my life today.

Today I will look at a mistake I have made, and discover what I can learn from it.

Today I will appreciate the outdoors with all of my senses.

Today I will tell the people in my life how much I love them.

I have what it takes to be a fabulous friend.

I am a miracle from head to toe.

Today I will start something I've been putting off by taking small steps at a time

I will reach out to someone with kindness today.

Daily Sayings

I will put all my energy into the present today, rather than the past or future.

My thoughts help to make my world what it is.

I will notice how I use my time today.

If I respect myself, I have inner wealth!

Today I will celebrate something great about myself that only I know about!

Today I will do my best to stay calm and relaxed all day long.

Today I will flex my mental muscles to keep my brain fit!

Today I will see the greatness in myself and others.

Today I will take the ordinary and make it extraordinary!

Asking questions keeps my mind sharp and alert.

My friends are among my greatest treasures.

Today I will take five minutes to imagine a peaceful world.

A smile is something that everyone says in the same language.

Most people agree - The greatest gifts are those that come from the heart.

Thinking positively is a great way to start the day!

I will eat healthy foods to stay healthy.

Everyone has the same basic need to love and be loved.

Daily Sayings

 Today I will see the beauty in everyone I meet.

 When I give to others, I gain even more myself.

 Today I will look for the hero in myself and others.

 I am loved for who I am rather than what I do.

 Today I will read something enjoyable for at least half an hour.

 A great day is made up of putting each hour to good use!

 Today is a day to begin to make a dream come true.

 Taking one action is worth a thousand words.

 Most of what I fear is just that – fear!

 Of all of the fun things there are to do, one of the best is trying something new.

 My brain is the greatest invention ever made!

 Today I will use my own inner genius.

 When I circle myself with excellence, I glow from the inside out!

 Today I will inspire myself by doing something creative for someone else.

 My life's journey is full of adventures, fun, and challenges.

 Both new and old friends have value!

Chapter 6

PARENT CONFERENCING

As every educator knows, we do not work in a vacuum. Our students only spend a few hours a day with us and the remainder of the time they are experiencing life with their families in many different ways. The quickest method of information-seeking is to ask the question directly to the source. Parent conferences offer us a chance to see body language, facial expressions, and voice intonations. Often, we are rewarded with insight that can better help us teach our students!

Included in this chapter is a role play activity to help teachers practice different scenarios that they may experience during parent conferences. Also included are tips for teachers when conferencing with parents, as well as a parent contact sheet that teachers can use to keep up with each time a teacher makes contact with a parent.

Faculty Activity

Faculty Handouts

WHAT DO YOU DO?
Role-Playing Activity

Purpose: This activity will help teachers practice and prepare for different scenarios that may occur during parent conferences.

Materials: Timer, Scenario Cards (pages 38-40)

Procedures: Facilitator makes copies of the Scenario Cards. There should be enough copies to have one card for every two people involved in the activity. Cards should be folded in half so that one side shows the "Scenario Description" and the other side shows the "Scenario Suggestions."

Participants choose a partner. Each pair chooses a Scenario Card that describes a parent conference. Have both partners read only the "Scenario Description" on the front of the card. One person plays the teacher and the other person plays the parent. The person playing the parent can be as challenging as he / she likes. Obviously, these scenes are meant to bring up sticky situations.

The facilitator sets the timer for three to five minutes. When the timer goes off, the two are to then discuss what took place and the problems they encountered. After the role play flip over the Scenario Card and read the "Scenario Suggestions." If need be, have them replay the scenario implementing the suggestions on the card.

SCENARIO CARDS

SCENARIO DESCRIPTION #1

A parent comes in 30 minutes late to the conference. The parent is obviously annoyed and distressed. What do you do?

SCENARIO SUGGESTIONS #1

The main thing you want to convey is concern. Ask the parent if everything is all right and if there is something you can do. If there is another parent waiting, politely tell the late parent that you are sorry for whatever happened and maybe the two of you could speak on the phone or reschedule. Make sure the parent knows that you are still interested in meeting with him/her. Do NOT keep the next parent waiting.

WHAT DO YOU DO?
SCENARIO CARDS

SCENARIO DESCRIPTION #2

A parent is very nice. He/She nods yes to everything you say and agrees with any suggestions that you give. How do you get him/her to open up?

SCENARIO SUGGESTIONS #2

Use open-ended questions with this type of parent. Try not to ask questions that will require just a yes or no answer. Ask the parent to share with you the concerns he/she has about the student. Ask him/her what kinds of things work at home to motivate and encourage the child. Elicit their input and thank them when they offer any type of feedback. It may be that they are feeling intimidated or overwhelmed.

SCENARIO DESCRIPTION #3

A parent is quick to blame the school, you, another student, and/or anyone except his/her child. How do you respond?

SCENARIO SUGGESTIONS #3

If a parent begins the conference negatively at least try and talk with him/her as you would the others by starting out with something positive. When you get into concerns, etc. about the child and the parent begins the blaming game listen to his/her concerns. Do not argue because this will only intensify the parent's temper. Remind the parent that the conference is really to talk about the child and specific educational concerns he/she might have. If a parent is verbally abusive to you DO NOT just sit there. Suggest taking a break and go and get the principal or assistant principal. DO NOT go back in and meet with the parent one on one. At this point you need some support! Do not be afraid to go to your principal. That is what he/she is there for. He/She does not expect you to take any sort of abuse from a parent. The principal is there to support you!

WHAT DO YOU DO?
SCENARIO CARDS

SCENARIO DESCRIPTION #4

A parent is very demeaning when talking about his/her child and has nothing positive to say. How do you handle this situation?

SCENARIO SUGGESTIONS #4

This type of parent rarely says anything nice. That is why you want to make sure that you start the conference off with something positive about the child. If he/she puts down the child and complains, share with the parent that you hear what he/she is saying and these concerns are things that you can help the child work on. It is a judgment call. If a parent continues to talk harshly about the child make sure you do check-ins with the child and speak with the counselor and principal as soon as possible.

SCENARIO DESCRIPTION #5

A parent has never shown up for a scheduled conference, is never home when you used to call until the phone was disconnected, and now there is no other phone numbers listed. In addition, the child walks to and from school so you are never able to catch a parent before or after school. However, you have been "encouraged" to make some sort of contact.

SCENARIO SUGGESTIONS #5

There is always one in every classroom! Although it is extremely frustrating for you, imagine what the home must be like. Sometimes we have to step back and think about what children go home to everyday. The teacher's goal is to get homework done and assignments completed. However, some families might be trying to find a place to sleep for the night or money for groceries. If you cannot get in touch with a parent get with your counselor. The counselor can go out to the house or get a social worker involved that might be able to track down the family. You are not alone! Use your resources. Sometimes the only way to communicate with a parent is through daily notes home in an agenda or folder. You are not expected to perform miracles! The only thing that is being asked is for you to make a concentrated effort to get in touch with the parent. Make sure you document every attempt, in addition to contacting the counselor for assistance. Don't be afraid to talk with your principal to get some additional suggestions.

Parent Conferencing Tips

From the Beginning

Not only do you want to start a parent conference with something positive about the child, you also want to sincerely thank the parent for coming in and acknowledge that it was hard for him / her to get off of work, find a babysitter, or whatever the situation may be and you appreciate their time.

Plan of Action

Do not go in and try to wing it. Have a plan. Jot down the things that you would like to address. Make sure that you include a chance for the parents to share their concerns. At the end of the conference go over the things that were addressed just for clarification and make sure that they know how much you appreciate their effort in their child's education.

Team Effort

When conferencing with the parent present the task of their child's education as a team effort. Without them you could not do your job. You are depending on them to reinforce the lessons that their child is learning in the classroom. If you give them some ownership in it they are more likely to buy into it and want to help.

Language

Remember to think before you speak. Your body language has A LOT to do with how the parent is going to react. Avoid crossing your arms or sitting behind a desk. Sit next to the parent. Your tone of voice is also important. Be precise with what you say and stay calm! Do not look away when the parent is talking. Have eye contact at all times.

Attitude

Last, make sure you go in and leave with a positive attitude. If you are frustrated or upset about something the parent WILL pick up on it. Remember: Attitudes are CONTAGIOUS!!!

Always begin a conference with something positive. You want the parent to feel at ease. It will encourage the parent to participate in the conference and share concerns.

PARENT CONTACTS THROUGHOUT THE YEAR

Send home a weekly newsletter.

Send notes home through an
agenda / folder.

Mail two positive notes a week.

Invite parents to come observe when students are having a writing party
or giving presentations.

PTA night-Going to PTA meeting is a great place. Not just during your
grade level but others as well. Chances are your students have siblings
and parents who may be there to see the brother or sister perform!

PTA sponsored nights at places like a fast food restaurant or pizza place.

Make contact with at least one parent a week with something positive.
It will pay off when you have something not so positive to share!

Post your weekly calendar / newsletter on your
school's website. Invite parents to contact
you via email.

PARENT CONTACT SHEET

Date	Name	+ OR -	REASON FOR CONTACT	OUTCOME
8/4/05	John Smith	+	Passed benchmark	Mother is pleased at progress student is making.

Chapter 7
· · · · · · · · · · · · · ·

20 SIMPLE TIPS FOR HOME TO HELP STUDENTS ACHIEVE

The following tips can be used as parent handouts at conferences or meetings throughout the year as the need arises. This could also be a great PTA meeting program. Parents are always looking for ways that are easy and user-friendly! The simple 20 tips give the parents a way to interact and help their child to succeed in the everyday tasks of school. It is true that we all have experienced different styles of child rearing in our own personal lives. Learning a new way to say or do something might make all the difference in the world when we are working with our kids.

Parent Handout

Tips for Student Achievement

Hassle-Free Homework

1. Don't banish your child to his room to study alone. If he prefers, let him work in the same room with you, while you read or do chores.

2. Suggest that your child start on the toughest subject first, while his energy level is high. It is usually more successful than starting with an easy task.

3. It is a big mistake to do your child's homework for him. Take the extra time to explain how he can do it instead. That way, he will learn from both the successes and mistakes.

Sticking with It

4. Teach your child how to talk to herself positively when concentration lags. Instead of, "I'll never finish this chapter," the thought might be "Only 6 more pages to go - I can make it."

5. Suggest a 5-10 minute activity break before your child tires of studying. Arm-wrestling or a run in the backyard will clear the head and help learning sink in.

6. Encourage your child to respect deadlines - she will have to cope with them throughout her life. Use rewards (not bribes) when appropriate. If she finishes on time, play a favorite game.

Make the Most of Reading

7. Have your child silently preview material before he begins reading the text. Notice headings, introductions, summaries, review questions, and charts.

8. Teach your child to use the diagramming technique. Chart the main idea in the passage and supporting details as the hub and spokes of a wheel.

9. Teach your child to use memory tricks. Look together for ways to associate the unknown with the known. For instance, the initials for the Great Lakes spells HOMES (Huron, Ontario, Michigan, Erie, and Superior).

Tips for Student Achievement

Enriching Experiences

10. Make it a point to have family meals together and discuss current events. Have a dictionary, globe, and an encyclopedia handy for reference.

11. Develop listening skills at home that can help in the classroom. Here is one way: Have family members close their eyes for two minutes and discuss every sound that they heard.

12. While solving puzzles or playing games, show your child how to use mental strategies, such as finding patterns, categorizing, guessing and checking, and making charts.

13. Make the kitchen a learning lab. Have your child read the steps of the recipe. Teach fractions with measuring spoons and cups, or cut a potato in half and fourths!

14. Use the TV as a learning tool. Make TV programs a jump off point to research ideas at the library. Also, show how commercials try to manipulate the masses.

15. Make the most of family travel time. Do crossword puzzles. Play Twenty Questions. Make up stories that can be continued by another family member. Count out of state license plates and find all 50!

Motivation: The Don'ts

16. Don't interrogate your child about what goes on at school as soon as he walks in the door - he is likely to regard it as an intrusion. Share something about your own day and wait for the child to follow the role modeling.

17. Never offer bribes for better performance. Don't give extra allowance for a good report card, or withhold allowance for a poor one. It simply confuses the issue.

18. Don't threaten - the tactic is ineffective. "If you don't pass, I'll ground you for a week" puts YOU, rather than your child, in control.

19. Don't take credit for your child's achievements. Instead of "I knew you could do it," say, "I'll bet you are proud of your hard work!"

20. Don't constantly push your child to top his previous achievements. If success brings pressure, your youngster may find it easier to fail!

Chapter 8

STUDY SKILLS

Assuming that we all come to school knowing how to memorize and use study skill tools is a false assumption! If we had photographic memories, we could do away with tests and measurement tools. Of course, we'd also be out of a teaching job! The following activity and handouts are provided to assist the teacher and parent in presenting the needed study skills in order to increase success in the classroom.

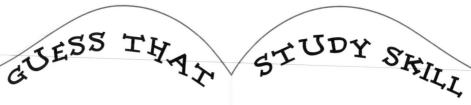

GUESS THAT STUDY SKILL

Name: _____   Date: _____

1. Work that has been assigned at school but is done at home is called...

— — — — — — — — —

2. To check for understanding after each chapter or unit, the teacher gives a ...

— — — —

3. If I have everything in the right place, I am showing...

— — — — — — — — — — — —

4. We go to school and study to...

— — — — —

5. If I am not listening in class, then I am not ....

— — — — — — — — — — — — — — —

6. If I want to make good grades, I have to...

— — — — — —

7. In order for me to understand the teacher's lesson, I have to ....

— — — — — —

8. In order for me to master a new concept, it will take ....

— — — — — — — —

9. If I am keeping up with my assignments and completing my work, I am showing ...

— — — — — — — — — — — — — —

10. Doing exactly what the teacher asked is called...

— — — — — — — — — — — — — — — — — —

Why We Need to Teach Study Skills

The first thing you need to remember and ALWAYS keep in mind is not to ASSUME anything.

You need to treat the beginning of the year as a refresher and practice of good study skills. If you teach the really young ones you may be the first to teach them. The older ones have been taught some but you want to re-teach and have them practice. Students learn by example.

Role-playing and modeling are the two best ways to teach your students good study skills, along with lots and lots of encouragement and patience.

You are building the minds of life-long learners. They are going to take what you teach them and apply those skills for years to come.

When you think of study skills such as organization, paying attention, and having a quiet place to work, you might think that these things should already be known. However, keep in mind that your classroom is much different than what the students may have encountered the year before. Keep in mind what home might be like for some kids. Organization and a quiet place may be the last two things that are considered in some homes.

DON'T FORGET TO USE YOUR
STUDY SKILLS

1. LISTEN

2. PAY ATTENTION

3. ASK QUESTIONS

4. STUDY

5. FOLLOW DIRECTIONS

6. DO YOUR HOMEWORK

Homework Strategies for the Working Parent

It is hard trying to come home after a long day at work to find that your daughter or son has four pages of homework. Don't forget, your child had a long day just like you! Homework time can be a bonding experience with you and your child or it can be an absolute nightmare. Here are some tips that might make things a little easier.

If your child goes to an after-school center instruct them to start their homework there. Getting it started and then finishing it at home will be much easier than trying to begin it after dinner. If a child is home with an older sibling, the same rule applies. They should start their homework and work on it for at least 30 minutes before putting it aside and going out to play. You are sending a message that even though you are not at home their studies are important and should be taken seriously.

You should have a schedule when you get home to help plan the evening. If you get home at 5:00 and dinner is at 6:00 then designate a time for you and your child to sit down to review and complete homework assignments. Homework is a way for students to practice independently and to let the parent know what the child is learning in school. Sometimes having homework time before dinner is better than after. You are the expert on your child and you know when he / she is most alert and attentive.

Make sure that there are no distractions. The T.V. should be off, no social calls should be taken or made, and other members of the family should not be in the same room doing other things. Some kids work well with soft background music, more specifically music that is instrumental only. Music by the latest pop star is most likely not homework appropriate.

Choose a special place for you and your child to go during homework time. It can be just a corner in the den or kitchen but it tells the child that it is your place.

Use this time to encourage your child. Their self esteem has a lot to do with how hard they will try. If they think they can they often will. Use phrases like, "Look at that, you did it." or "Wow, you figured it out!" or "Look at that smile, you must be proud." You want to give the child ownership of the accomplishment.

Don't hesitate to contact the teacher if you do not understand an assignment. Write a note in your child's folder or agenda or send him / her an email. He / She will appreciate it and be happy to explain!!

Things to Remember When Assigning Homework

Homework needs to be given only to check for understanding. It is not a punishment but a way to verify the learning.

Assignments should not take longer than 15 minutes for Kindergarten and 1st grade, 20 minutes for 2nd and 3rd grade, and 30 minutes for 4th and 5th grade. Middle school students are usually faced with multiple classes and homework can take 1-2 hours.

Homework should keep the student's attention. It should be an assignment that can be done independently.

Know that others are involved with the homework process in some homes, but many children have no one to supervise these activities.

If you are consistent with assignment days for certain subjects, this might be a great communication tool for a busy family in the evenings.

Always take the time to evaluate the assignments that you give ... it is a way to correct errors in the learning process and to attach worth to the project.

Chapter 9
· · · · · · · · · · · ·

CELEBRATING DIVERSITY

Diversity includes an infinite range of individuals' unique characteristics and experiences, such as communication styles, career, work, life experience, educational backgrounds and other variables. This is in addition to differences based on ethnicity, gender, age, religion, disability, national origin and sexual orientation. In the schools, we are given the opportunity to have many chances to celebrate and recognize individual differences and styles. Each classroom seems to be a melting pot offering an eclectic environment in which to experience tolerance and acceptance. The more we find our differences, the more we see how alike we really are as a people! Children are curious, but they usually accept others by their character traits, not by preconceived notions. Let's be an example to our students and let them judge for themselves by personal experience!

CELEBRATING OUR DIFFERENCES

Purpose: This activity can be used with faculty members to reinforce the idea that individual styles and differences should be recognized and celebrated.

Materials: Small bags of each type of M&M® candies: PLAIN, PEANUT, ALMOND, and PEANUT BUTTER, chart paper or overhead, markers and paper

Procedures: Show each type of candy to the group. Have them separate into small groups according to their preferences. Ask them to create a short ad or commercial that would best convince someone to choose their candy. Give 5 minutes for each group to either create a poster, play or song that includes every group member. Enjoy the creativity and be sure to give proper kudos to each group after their presentation. When all four are complete, write the following questions on the overhead or chart paper for discussion.

1. **Did the group use the tactic of "putting down" the other types of candy to make theirs appear better?**

2. **Did they make statements that their candy was "the best" or better than the others?**

3. **Were there false claims of superiority?**

4. **How do people generally make choices?**

5. **Can we ever come to a unanimous conclusion as to the BEST candy in the groups?**

6. **Do you see that differences are encouraged in order to satisfy the broad tastes of each individual?**

SOUNDS LIKE WE CAN ALL LEARN THAT DIFFERENCES ARE GOOD!!!

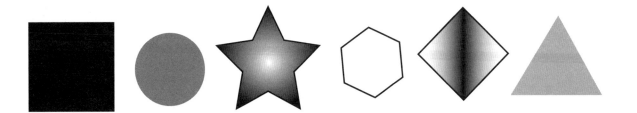

Differences We Should See

As one looks across North America, one thing noticeable is its uniqueness. We are a varied group of different ethnic backgrounds. Within each city, you can find specialty grocery stores, restaurants, and churches that cater to the preferences that we were accustomed to as we grew up. The "melting pot" is a descriptive way to illustrate the many different cultures that have made North America their new home.

In our American society, we treasure freedom and the right to express our ideas. With this in mind, it makes perfect sense to take some time to learn about the lives, ideals, and cultures of the varied different groups among us.

Schools are a perfect venue to teach these unique differences through the celebration of cultures and their special contributions to our society.

There is comfort in knowledge!

LEARN ABOUT US!

NAME: _____   DATE: _____

Try to fill in the blanks finding two answers for each topic. Use an encyclopedia, the internet, books, or other resources to help you complete this chart. A few blanks have been filled in for you. Share the information you find with others.

	African American	Asian American	European American	Hispanic American	Native American
FOOD			Sausage & Sauerkraut		
HOLIDAY		Chinese New Year			
CONTRIBUTION TO AMERICA	Cotton Gin				
FAMOUS AMERICAN				Juan Seguin	

TEACHING BY EXPERIENCES

Culture is the total of all the different ways that we live our daily lives. It encompasses the beliefs, customs and values of our family and friends. It is a special way that can guide us in our behaviors that we express in our local group. It is often our language or the way that we choose to communicate. It also assists in forming early patterns of thinking!

The problem that we face is that we often do not understand the customs of those who differ from us. We sometimes fall into the dangerous pitfall of stereotyping groups and not looking at each person as an individual. We use selective perceptions and fixed ideas because of past experiences or information, not always truth based.

Experience often changes our perception and level of comfort around things that are different. It is helpful to have a chance to experience Braille or experiences that mimic learning disabilities or hearing impairments. We can appreciate only if we "Walk a mile in another's shoes!"

Do you have any first thoughts when these words are expressed?

NEW YORKER--CALIFORNIAN

WOMEN--MEN--GIFTED--DISABLED

ELDERLY--OBESE-- HOMELESS

Chapter 10

WORKING WITH THE ESL STUDENT

Schools are becoming more and more diverse. Teachers and staff are challenged each day with making sure that EVERY child, no matter what language they speak, gets the education that will carry him/ her through college and into adulthood. Included in this chapter is a fun activity that can be done in the classroom that will get students conversing in a non-threatening way. Also included are tips for teachers to keep in mind when working with an E.S.L. student, and some ways that schools can show an appreciation for these students and their families.

Student Activity

Faculty Handouts

School-Wide Activities

RESTAURANT DINING

Purpose: This activity is a fun way to get students talking and conversing in basic, every-day language.

Material: Menus from various, local restaurants

Procedures: First, brainstorm with the class the experience of going into a restaurant or fast food place and what goes on. Talk about having to explain to the waiter or employee what you want and make sure that he / she understands so that your food will be correct. Discuss what types of things are ordered such as an appetizer, main course, drink, side dishes, a dessert. Go over what all of these mean. Some students may not understand what a side dish is or if a salad comes with dressing, what "dressing" is. Touch on the importance of eye contact, speaking slowly and listening. Going over a basic greeting is useful as the employee will surely greet the customer and the customer (student) will need to respond.

Next, have the students get in groups of three. Distribute menus from local restaurants around town. Have the students look it over and ask any questions that they may have. Have each group select one student to be the customer, one to be the employee and the other to be a bystander. The "bystander" listens to the other two group members role play and then offers feedback. Students then rotate roles. Role plays should continue until everyone has been each role twice. When everyone is finished role playing, come back as a class and discuss good things that happened and also questions that may have come up during the role plays.

Follow-Up: To make it even more challenging, find menus that are in different languages.

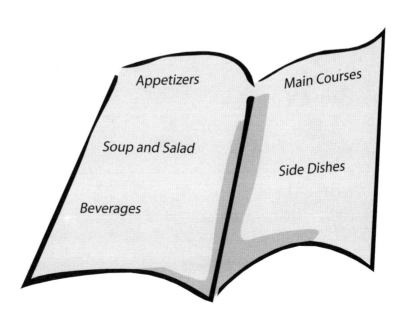

WORKING WITH E.S.L. STUDENTS

All teachers may have E.S.L. students in their classroom. Just because you are not an E.S.L. teacher does not mean you won't have one or even several. Some E.S.L. students are in regular classrooms due to the parent denying services. It is up to you to make the classroom a learning environment for both English-speaking and your E.S.L. student(s).

Buddy up your E.S.L. student with a classmate that can make sure that instructions and assignments are written down and understood.

Never assume an E.S.L. student understands. Always make sure by asking questions and explaining directions in short, easy-to-understand vocabulary.

Use visual media and manipulatives to support your instruction. This will help in understanding material more clearly.

When you are explaining something, remember that your E.S.L. students are processing what you are saying. It is like you hearing something in another language and trying to understand it in English. Speak clearly and slowly. (Often times teachers get carried away with a lesson and get excited and this speeds up the speech.) Just be aware of the rate of your speech.

When your E.S.L. students are just learning English and are practicing speaking, try not to correct them when they do not pronounce a word correctly. They will eventually learn the correct way to say something through you and others modeling those words. If you make it a point to let them know they are wrong, you may inadvertently isolate them and make them feel self-conscious about speaking English.

The most important thing you can do as a teacher is offer a classroom that feels safe and secure for learning and trying new things.

THINGS TO KEEP IN MIND

Many times teachers and staff misinterpret a child's behavior as defiant or rude when in actuality it's simply something they are doing that is within their culture. Keep in mind the following behaviors when you are working with E.S.L. students.

Some cultures, place more emphasis on the family, rather than the individual. A child may be out of school to take care of a sick sibling or parent. Food and shelter are often more important than education.

Often you will notice parents from other cultures that nod at everything you say, seeming to agree. Do not assume this. In fact, they may not understand what you are saying. The nodding is a way of respect that they are paying attention. Make sure a translator is on hand to communicate with the parent.

Some cultures have a diet that is rich in certain oils and ingredients like garlic that create an unpleasant smell that is secreted through the skin, much like the smell that people give off when their diet consists of almost no carbohydrates and all protein. Because this odor is unpleasant, student's may be ridiculed or made fun of.

In many cultures maintaining eye contact with an authority figure is considered disrespectful and rude. E.S.L. students may also call the teacher "Teacher" or "Miss" as a form of respect.

In some cultures, parents may not have much confidence in the "female" educator. Women in these cultures traditionally are not the decision-maker or authority figure and boys and their fathers may reflect these feelings to you if you are a female teacher.

Some E.S.L. children often do well academically when it comes to math and subjects where memorizing things are important. These children are typically very good readers but can usually only decode the words. There is little to no comprehension due to the child not having yet mastered the English language.

Taking these points into consideration will help you in your relationship with both the student and the parent. When in doubt ask a parent about their culture. They will appreciate your interest and be thankful that you didn't assume that their child was being rude or disrespectful!

ALL AROUND THE WORLD BULLETIN BOARD

Purpose: This activity shows appreciation for your ESL students and their families by recognizing and providing information on the countries native to them.

Materials: Large world map, pushpins, information and "pin-ups" relating to various countries native to your students

Procedures: Set up a bulletin board somewhere in your school where there is a high amount of student and parent traffic. The bulletin board is designed to recognize the countries that your students are from. At the beginning of the school year, place a large world map on the bulletin board and mark with pushpins the countries that are native to your students and/or their families. Once all represented countries are marked, research can begin on the various places. Each month (or every couple of weeks, depending on your E.S.L. population), a certain country can be spotlighted. The students from that country are given an opportunity to share with their class and others classes if they choose, how life is there compared to the United States (ie. the food that is eaten, the culture, and the education taught). This process makes the E.S.L. students feel more comfortable and part of the class/school. It also educates everyone else, including the staff!!

Follow-Up: An extension would be to have family members come in and speak or share things with the class. If the family member does not speak English they are still welcome. The student can usually help. Teaching the English-speaking students words from their native language is always a favorite and a highlight of the E.S.L. student's experience!!!

MULTICULTURAL NIGHT

Purpose: This activity spotlights many different cultures. Students, staff, parents, and other community members can come and enjoy authentic food, while learning about each country.

Materials: Cultural displays made by students, authentic cultural foods made by parents and / or community members, a table for each country represented

Procedures: Set up a night to spotlight many different cultures, not just the ones that represent your school. Each country is given a space with a table and any visual equipment needed. The event can be held in the school cafeteria or auditorium. The teachers sign up for a country and then volunteers from the community and parents sign up to help. Research is done by students and displays are made. Parents and community members pitch in by making food and offering to be the speaker for the table on the night of the event. It is an awesome sight to see parents and family members of some of these countries come in native clothing and share their experiences. Tables may be displayed with samples of foods, clothing, photos, and artifacts from that country.

Chapter 11

CHILD ABUSE ISSUES

This chapter pertains to issues that concern the proper handling of child abuse. Obtain a copy of local policies and procedures that are in place in your particular school district. Usually, a yearly in-service is required to refresh all staff members in their responsibility to uphold the law where child abuse is involved. We can not afford to let one child's cries go unheard. *"The Hurt"* by Teddi Doleski and *"A Safe Place to Live"* by Michelle Harrison are excellent short books for discussion and can be used in activities with any age group.

THE HURT

Purpose: This activity can be shared with adults or children to remind them how important it is to not keep their "hurts" to themselves.

Material: *The book, The Hurt* by Teddi Doleski

Procedures: Take five minutes to read aloud the book, *The Hurt*, to the audience. It is a child's book that has a very profound effect on adults. It is not directly about abuse but the tragic truth is that many children and adults suffer because they keep the issue of abuse a secret. The underlying truth is that we need to not keep our hurts to ourselves & nurse them until they grow out of our control. As with abuse, keeping the secret only allows the pain and hurt to continue and destroy our lives.

Ask for each person to take a minute and think of the one hurt that they have kept or are currently keeping. Explain that we all need to find a way to let these hurts go. You can write about it, discuss it with a friend, or find a counselor.

ABUSE FACTS*

National Facts

- In 2001, about 3,844,000 children were reported as possible victims of child abuse and neglect in the United States.

- Of those cases confirmed, 54 percent were neglect, 19 percent were physical abuse, 10 percent were sexual abuse, 3 percent were emotional maltreatment, and 14 percent were due to other forms of maltreatment.

Every Second

- Every 11 seconds a child is reported abused or neglected.

- Every 5 minutes a child is arrested for a violent crime.

- Every 17 minutes a baby dies.

- Every 2 hours a child is a homicide victim.

* adapted from Texas Department of Protective and Regulatory Services

ABUSE FACTS*

Daily Facts

- 4 children die from child abuse every day.

- 27 children die from poverty every day.

- 689 babies are born with inadequate prenatal care every day.

- 13,700 children are abused and neglected.

Outcome Abuse

Total Physical Abuse:

- 60-70% of abused children suffer bruises and welts.

- 15-20% suffer skeletal injury.

- 25-30% of cases involve brain or neuromotor dysfunction.

Social Abuse:

- 50% of runaway youth have been physically abused and an even greater percentage have been sexually abused.

- 60% of prostitutes were sexually abused as children.

- 65% of prison inmates at the Ferguson Unit (TDC) were abused as children.

- 90% of convicted murderers were physically abused as children.

* adapted from National Center for Injury Prevention and Control

ABUSE FACTS*

Outcome Abuse... continued

Emotional & Psychological:

- 50% of abused children have school-related problems.

- 22% of abused children suffer learning disorders requiring special education.

- 60-80% of adult drug and alcohol abusers have a history of child abuse.

Reporting Abuse

- An oral report must be made immediately (within 48 hours) to nearest Child Protective Service Office, to the 24-hour Child Abuse Hotline (1-800-252-5400), or to the local law enforcement officials. As a follow-up, a written report must be made to the Department of Protective & Regulatory Services within five days. Anyone who files a report is immune from civil or criminal liablity - if the report is made in "good faith" and "without malice."

- "Good faith" means that the person took reasonable steps to learn the facts that were readily available and at hand.

- "Without malice" means that the person did not intend to injure or violate the rights of another person.

* adapted from National Center for Injury Prevention and Control

TYPES OF DISCLOSURE

Children often feel that it is too painful or dangerous to disclose the fact that someone has sexually abused them. It could be that they do not even have the words or the knowledge to express the injustice that they feel. Of course, it would be so much easier if the child were to directly tell us what has been happening and that they want help! Unfortunately that doesn't usually happen.

Sometimes abused children give *vague hints* such as; "My uncle always sleeps in my bed when he comes over." "I think Mr. Man, my neighbor, wears funny kinds of underwear." "My babysitter plays yucky games when my brother is not at home." When children share these kinds of statements, it is because they are wanting someone to listen or to ask specific questions that might help them to share the information that could free them from the abuse. They may either be embarrassed, scared, or confused about telling details until they know they can trust the grown-up.

There are other times that an abused child will try to *disguise* the information; "My sister said that she knows a girl who is being touched in her private area." "What should a girl do if she tells her Mom that she had to see a dirty movie and she doesn't believe her?" We might not know if the child is really talking about a friend or about herself. This is the time to encourage the child to tell you more through open questions or other play activities. This hopefully will encourage the child to trust you with more information.

Abused children may also try to *impose restrictions* on your actions when they share with you in confidence. "I'll tell you something, but you have to promise that you won't tell my Dad." "I need to tell you something, but I'll get in big trouble if anyone knows I said something." These are red flags. Most children are very aware that if they break the silence which covers the abuse, they may have to deal with negative consequences. The abusers often use threats to keep the child silent. It is important that the child knows before disclosure that you are there to help and will need to confidentially share information with people directly involved in the legal process in order to keep him/her safe.

Here are a few things to do to help a child be more comfortable as you listen to their story.

  * *Speak in a private location.*
  * *Don't express facial shock.*
  * *Let them know you believe them.*
  * *Use the child's vocabulary.*
  * *Tell them they have a right to tell an adult.*
  * *Reassure them that they are not bad and not at fault.*
  * *Let them know what you are going to do.*
  * *Report to Child Protective Services.*

We are not responsible to investigate these situations. Our duty is to report and get the child protected. You can be their lifeline for the future.

PHYSICAL AND BEHAVIORAL INDICATORS OF ABUSE AND NEGLECT

Physical Abuse

PHYSICAL INDICATORS	BEHAVIORAL INDICATORS
Unexplained Bruises and Welts - on face, lips, mouth - on torso, back, buttocks, thighs - in various stages of healing - clustered, forming regular patterns - reflecting shape of article used to inflict - electric cord, belt buckle, shoeprint - on several surface areas **Unexplained Burns** - cigar, cigarette burns, especially on soles of feet, palms, backs - immersion burns - sock like, glove-like, donut-shaped on buttocks or genitalia - patterns like iron tip, electric burners - rope burns on arms, legs, neck or torso **Unexplained Fractures** - to skull, nose, facial structure - in various stages of healing - multiple fractures	**Wary of Adult Contacts** **Apprehensive When Other Children Cry** **Behavioral Extremes** - aggressiveness - withdrawal **Afraid to Go Home After School** **Frightened of Parent** **Verbally Mimicking Anger in Play** (younger children) **Poor Peer Interactions** **Reports Cases of Injury by Adults**

The best way to help is to listen! Do your part to save our kids!

* adapted from Institute for Clinical Systems Improvement. *Recognizing child abuse and neglect.* Bloomington, MN (1997)
Available: http://www.new-life.net/chldsaf4.htm

PHYSICAL AND BEHAVIORAL INDICATORS OF ABUSE AND NEGLECT

Sexual Abuse

PHYSICAL INDICATORS	*BEHAVIORAL INDICATORS*
Difficulty in Walking or Sitting	Unwilling to Change for Gym Class or Participate
Torn, Stained or Bloody Underclothes	Withdrawal
Pain or Itching in Genital Area	Fantasy or Infantile Behavior
Bruising or Bleeding in External Genitalia - vaginal or anal	Bizarre, Sophisticated or Unusual Sexual Behavior or Knowledge
Venereal Disease - especially in preteens	Poor Peer Relationships
Excessive Public Masturbation	Dressing in Clothes That Are Inappropriate
Pregnancy	Delinquent or "Run Away"
	Reports Sexual Assault by Caregiver or Other

The best way to help is to listen! Do your part to save our kids!

* adapted from Institute for Clinical Systems Improvement. *Recognizing child abuse and neglect.* Bloomington, MN (1997)
Available: http://www.new-life.net/chldsaf4.htm

PHYSICAL AND BEHAVIORAL INDICATORS OF ABUSE AND NEGLECT

Emotional Abuse

PHYSICAL INDICATORS	*BEHAVIORAL INDICATORS*
Speech Disorders Lags in Physical & Social Development Failure to Thrive Anxiety	**Habit Disorders** - sucking - biting - rocking - self-injurious behavior **Conduct Disorders** - antisocial - destructive **Neurotic Traits** - sleep disorders - inhibition to play **Psychoneurotic Reactions** - hysteria - depression - phobia - attempted suicide

The best way to help is to listen! Do your part to save our kids!

* adapted from Institute for Clinical Systems Improvement. *Recognizing child abuse and neglect.* Bloomington, MN (1997)
Available: http://www.new-life.net/chldsaf4.htm

PHYSICAL AND BEHAVIORAL INDICATORS OF ABUSE AND NEGLECT

Physical Neglect

PHYSICAL INDICATORS	BEHAVIORAL INDICATORS
Constant Hunger	Begging for Food

Poor Hygiene	Extended Days at School
	  - often arrives early
	  - often leaves late

Poorly-Sized Clothes	
Constant Lack of Supervision	Constant Fatigue - sleeping in class
Unattended Physical or Medical Needs	Alcohol and Drug Use
Abandonment	Delinquency - thefts
	States That There is No Caretaker
	Lacks Sufficient Clothing for Weather

The best way to help is to listen! Do your part to save our kids!

* adapted from Institute for Clinical Systems Improvement. *Recognizing child abuse and neglect.* Bloomington, MN (1997)
Available: http://www.new-life.net/chldsaf4.htm

Chapter 12

SUICIDE PREVENTION ISSUES

One of the hardest issues to tackle is that of a suicide threat or suicide completion. The results leave everyone with doubts and questions. We all wonder what we might have done to prevent this situation... what did we miss. As a survivor, the guilt and confusion is wide spread and each person has a personal connection to the tragedy. Suicide is a desperate act that has lasting lifelong consequences for those left behind. The ideas shared here are just a way to awareness... not a means of understanding the reasons or choices of the suicidal person. Each case is different and each person's pain must be acknowledged and accepted. Included in this chapter are warning signs of suicidal behavior and also a form for personal documentation.

Faculty Handouts

Faculty Form

HOW TO HANDLE A SUICIDE THREAT

1. Take EVERY threat seriously.

2. Always refer the case to a competent professional for assistance.

3. Make sure that all weapons or dangerous materials are taken away.

4. Offer crisis intervention counseling.

5. Always call and notify parent / guardian or a trusted family member and set up an intervention plan.

6. Assure the person that they are not alone.

7. Never leave them without supervision.

HOW TO HANDLE A
SUICIDE ATTEMPT

1. Provide emergency first aid. Call 911 if you see that emergency care is needed.

2. Offer crisis counseling services.

3. Contact a parent or guardian and if an ambulance is not necessary, an administrator can provide transportation to the hospital.

4. If there are upset witnesses, request counseling help for them.

5. Refer family to a physician or mental health professional. If student goes to hospital, send a school representative to meet parents at the hospital.

6. Make a re-entry plan for the student that includes supportive counseling & follow up.

Suicide Attempt
Documentation Report

Student Name _____

School _____

Grade _____ Age _____ D.O.B. _____

Guardian _____ Relationship _____

Address _____

_____

Home Phone _____ Work/ Cell _____

Precipitating Events:

    A.

    B.

    C.

Behavior Warning Signs:

    A.

    B.

    C.

Action Plan:

WARNING SIGNS OF SUICIDE

VERBAL CLUES

Subtle or indirect statements that indicate a wish to die, of hopelessness and helplessness, ex. "I should never have been born." "No one cares if I live or die." "I hate living like this." Direct statements come right to the point. "I'm going to jump in front of a car." "I want to die." "I am going to kill myself."

BEHAVIORS

- Sadness and crying
- Isolation and withdrawal
- Disinterest in previous activities
- Drop in grades & lack of energy
- Inability to concentrate & apathy
- Change in sleeping or eating habits
- Neglect of personal hygiene or appearance
- Giving away possessions
- Taking unnecessary risks
- Saying good-bye
- Reoccurring death themes in art & writing

RISK FACTORS

- Loss of significant relationships, recent moves
- Family disruptions and stress
- Trouble with the law
- Poor communication/relationship with guardians
- Pressures in achievement
- Serious physical illness or mental illness
- Major disappointments, rejection or failure
- Parental dysfunction & suicidality
- Concern about sexual identity

HOW TO BE A GOOD LISTENER

During a highly intense conversation, it is critical to be in top form when you are offering an ear. Sometimes people tend to fall into patterns from their past. Some of us are lucky to have had wonderful experiences from those around us. When we needed someone they were there and attentive to our needs. Others of us are vulnerable to fall into the trap of... no one helped in my situation so I'll just send the crisis situation to somebody else! But, of course, it may be too late by that time. The following ideas can put us on equal footing and truly help to assist in the process of empathetic responses.

1. **Remove distractions, close door, turn off phone or T.V.**

2. **Focus on the speaker, maintain eye contact and listening position.**

3. **Allow for tears, silence, or processing time, these are very normal issues.**

4. **Paraphrase to show understanding. Sounds like you are feeling.... In other words.... What I hear you saying is...**

5. **Ask a question if you don't understand.**

6. **Be open, neutral, and supportive. Be careful of personal bias or prejudice...**

7. **Offer time and patience and seek help if needed.**

Chapter 13
• • • • • • • • • • • • •

DEALING WITH GRIEF

The following pages offer several different ideas assisting in the grief process that is part of all of our lives. If we become more comfortable ourselves, with the subject of loss, we can then be helpful to others. The tips and suggestions are a beginning of this learning process. Remember that all different types of reactions are normal for people. It is best not to be judgemental or impatient with a person dealng with one of the hardest experiences that life deals to us. Loss is a normal life experience and grief is a reaction to loss. We can all heal but we just need some facilitation. Children's understanding of death continually changes as they grow. They grieve through the common activity of play and acting out. They require a safe place to do this ... we can help!

WE CAN PICK UP THE PIECES

Purpose: This is a very therapeutic activity to share with families. They can work on this project together and spend some precious time communicating and reliving memories. It can be used for death, divorce, or loss by moving residences.

Materials: Clay flower pot (best if sprayed white), hammer, towel, several colored permanent markers, hot glue gun, glue sticks

Procedures: Confirm that it feels like everything has fallen apart since the divorce / death / move. You can then express this by breaking a clay flowerpot into several large pieces.

Be sure to wrap the pot in a towel to prevent accidents and place on a hard cement surface, like the sidewalk. Hit it firmly with a hammer. Be careful not to shatter it into bits. Each family member can be given a piece and asked to decorate the outside with a special memory that they'd like to share.

Since everyone has worked so hard to pick up the pieces, it is now time to fit the pieces together with a hot glue gun. Working together, have the family restore the pot. Even though it might look different now, it still can hold flowers again. All the breaks represent the scars in our hearts because we will always miss the way things once were. This process shows, in a physical way, that we can go on with our memories.

Life sometimes feels as though it can just fall apart ... but it doesn't and eventually with some hard work, we are able to put the pieces back together again.

A Child's Journey Through Grief
Starting to Deal with Anger

Name: _____ **Date:** _____

List 5 ways that are healthy ways to express anger:

1.

2.

3.

4.

5.

List 5 ways that are not OK to express anger:

1.

2.

3.

4.

5.

Briefly write about a time when you felt angry:

Draw what might happen if someone holds their anger inside and does not talk about it.

Ways to Remember and Honor Our Loved Ones

Wrap a box with examples of how the person was a gift to you.

Make or buy a special ornament for the Christmas Tree.

Make a scrapbook.

Look at favorite photo albums.

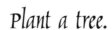

Create a memorial service.

Do something for someone in need.

Donate in the name of the loved one.

Plant a tree.

Carry a special keepsake.

Steps to Help a Child Through Loss

1. Talk about loss whenever a child asks questions.

2. Answer honestly and only what's asked.

3. Know that until they are about nine, they won't know that death is permanent.

4. Confirm that they did not cause this... sometimes they are confused by wishes.

5. Recommend that the parent / guardian take the child to a cemetery before death happens close to them.

6. Ask them what they wonder about.

7. Talk about your own feelings of sadness when you experienced death.

8. Don't wait for one complete "tell everything session."

Chapter 14

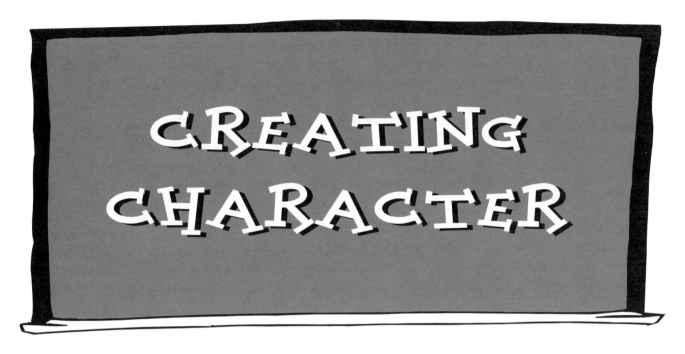

CREATING CHARACTER

The following chapter includes a fun bingo game that students can do that will promote conversation about character. It will get students thinking about the importance of having good character. This also helps adults see the most beneficial ways to model citizenship, respect, fairness, responsibility, caring, etc. Also included in this chapter are two faculty handouts that will get them thinking about their role in their students' lives. Often, it is not just as an educator! There is also a classroom pledge that students can say daily and a fun and quick faculty activity that can be done at any in-service or meeting just for the sake of giving out door prizes or lightening the mood. You can see which staff member comes prepared for anything!!!

What Kind of Character Do You Have?

Mingle and collect each other's names according to who matches each square.
See how many squares you can fill in.

Has picked up someone else's trash _____	Has done a favor for a friend _____	Has cried at a movie _____	Has donated money or items _____
Is not afraid to stand up for someone being picked on _____	Talks about their anger when they are upset _____	Walks away if others are talking badly about a friend _____	Has volunteered to read to a younger child _____
Will admit when they are wrong _____	Is not embarrassed to be friends with someone less popular _____	Is not afraid to say, "No!" _____	Has been really sorry for hurting someone else's feelings _____
Will do the right thing even when no one is watching _____	Would greet a new student and show him / her around _____	Has stolen and then admitted it and apologized _____	Always tries their best! _____

Children Learn What They Live

If a child lives with criticism, he learns to condemn.

If a child lives with hostility, she learns to fight.

If a child lives with ridicule, he learns to be shy.

If a child lives with shame, she learns to feel guilty.

If a child lives with tolerance, he learns to be patient.

If a child lives with encouragement, she learns confidence.

If a child lives with praise, he learns to appreciate.

If a child lives with fairness, she learns justice.

If a child lives with security, he learns to have faith.

If a child lives with approval, she learns to like herself.

If a child lives with acceptance and friendship, he learns to find love in the world.

- Author Unknown

Don't worry that children never listen to you. Worry that they are always watching you!

Robert Fulghum,
20th-Century
American Author

Classroom Pledge

I believe in me and my ability to do my best at all times.

I will respect myself and the rights of others.

I will take responsibility for my learning and the quality of my work.

Today I will be the best me I can be!

_____

Signature

WHAT DO YOU HAVE?

Purpose: This activity is a fun icebreaker for faculty members to demonstrate character traits in a meeting or other group session.

Procedures: Ask the participants to open their purses or pockets and be the first to produce the following items! Explain the character trait that each item reflects. Prizes can be given to the winners!

Paper Clip	You are organized
Driver's License	You love kids that drive you crazy
Aspirin/Tylenol	You never get stressed out
Kleenex	You dry up the tears
Chewing Gum	You keep things together
Candy	You are so sweet
Key	You are a key to education
Vitamin	You need care for the caregiver
Comb	You take care of messes
Credit Card	You are always charged up
Business Card	You help people keep in touch
Nuts/Crackers	You're a little nuts or crackers
Toy	You play around
Mirror	You look at the good side

Chapter 15
• • • • • • • • • • •

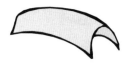

CAUSES OF MISBEHAVIOR

When we need help the most in dealing with misbehavior in the classroom, we don't need to be looking for books or chapters in order to get suggestions. These times that children challenge us always seem to put a kink in our day. This chapter provides a helpful booklet addressing frequent misbehaviors which take valuable time away from the learning process. Keeping this resource on your desk for quick reference will help facilitate immediate results. If we can find a solution in an instant ... learning will be the outcome!

Faculty Handouts

Issues That Promote Misbehavior

- Sibling rivalry
- Feels unloved at home and at school
- Pressured from expectations that are unattainable
- Discipline too harsh or inconsistent
- Too many failures - too few successes
- Physical & health reasons
- Bored
- Poor environmental stimulation
- Feels rejected by parents, teachers or peers
- Poor nutrition
- Has been "passed along" from grade to grade & knows it
- Is allowed to miss school often
- Poor parental attitude toward school
- Punished more than rewarded
- Deep-seated emotional problems
- Is the family scapegoat
- Feelings of hostility toward adults
- Lacks necessary material things
- Lack of home supervision
- No proper cleanliness in the home
- Dislikes teacher
- Brings problems from home & takes it out on school

THE CHILD WHO BITES, HITS AND KICKS

TRY: Making sure that the behavior no longer pays off
- by rewarding positive behavior
- by ignoring it if possible

Providing instructions about the use of
- punching bags, red flag signals, stretching to relieve tension
- talking time "What are we angry about?"

Using alternative activities for the classroom such as
- a clay/stress ball to help calm a stressful situation
- sand tray, timers, using a special cool-down place in the room

Keeping an anecdotal list of times the child exhibits actions

Avoiding confrontations that lead to actions

Asking his/ her help with another student quick to anger

THE CHILD WHO CHEATS AND STEALS

TRY: Removing reasons for cheating

- check instructional level
- change supervision and seating opportunities
- provide more space to work

Encouraging the child by

- using praise to build confidence
- use a policy of rewards for accomplishments
- put child in a position of trust "Watch these for me."

Talking to the child

- to find reason for this need
- help child see that their rights are protected by rules

THE CHILD WHO DESTROYS PROPERTY

TRY: Talking with the child to help him / her
- feel the need to respect property
- recognize the hard work behind the property
- recognize the feelings behind the act

Building confidence by
- using group recognition
- praising when the materials are used properly
- putting them in charge of the care of a piece of property

Providing settings where
- he / she can reason through feelings of aggression
- the item can be repaired or replaced by the child

THE CHILD WHO REFUSES TO DO ASSIGNED TASKS AT HOME OR SCHOOL

TRY: Rewarding for work that is completed by
- keeping a record of daily "work" average
- arranging with parents for home rewards
- using behavior modification sheet

Making assignments
- interesting, worthwhile, varied, and necessary
- a game when feasible
- which require verbal answers instead of written

Evaluating if child is capable of the work

Using the "buddy system" in class or on projects

Using interest centers for motivation

THE CHILD WHO BREAKS RULES AT SCHOOL

TRY: Examining the rules and
- see if they are necessary for learning and safety

Having the children take an active part in making the rules
- short, positive, easy to remember, few in number

Refusing to get trapped into
- arguing with the child about a rule
- making one exception after another

Anticipating actions & overcoming rule-breaking behavior by
- giving a certain number of passes to the restroom
- offering signs to indicate a need for a free time out
- staying cool, calm, & consistent

THE CHILD WHO CAN'T SIT STILL

TRY: Observing to find the details that surround the situation by
- seating the child close to you

Having the child checked for clothing problems, pinworms, or other health issues

Finding out when and what goes on at home or over weekends

Determining if assignments are too hard or too long

Using creative movements by
- acting out various concepts
- pantomiming story characters
- planning for a wiggle activity or exercise time

Eliminating or shifting materials that aggravate movement

THE CHILD WHO CRIES TOO EASILY

TRY: Establishing a closer relationship with the student by
- taking him / her aside to talk privately
- having the child sit somewhere else until ready to talk
- giving the child small tasks to build confidence
- providing a "magic stone" to think about or hold
- putting a note of encouragement in child's hand
- giving an envelope to put worries in and seal away

Being firm but do not stress the child by angry tones

Watching for signs that tears may begin and distract the child

Drawing or writing about insecurities

Seeking help in cases of unusual anxiety

THE CHILD WHO CAN'T FOLLOW DIRECTIONS

TRY: Determining if hearing is a problem

Standing in front and touching to reinforce contact

Starting with complete attention, ex. whistle or bell

Developing discrimination and listening skills by

- giving directions in phrases, avoiding excessive verbiage
- playing "Simon Says," "Password," "What's My Line?"
- assigning a "secretary" to take a message & respond
- tape recording 1, 2, & 3 step directions at a listening center

Post a schedule of classroom events and reward the prepared students

THE CHILD WHO DEMANDS TEACHER REASSURANCE

TRY: Building independence by
- teaching trial and error in problem-solving
- talking about sharing teacher's time
- giving child reassurances at fixed and specific times
- making a work contract
- giving simple tasks to be done independently

Looking for reasons for insecurity by
- letting the child write, draw or talk about insecurities

Assigning a buddy

Developing a non-threatening atmosphere, praising several small independent actions

THE CHILD WHO BULLIES

TRY: Communicating by
- having separate & combined discussions with child and class teaching the group not to reinforce aggression

Giving the child personal attention by
- re-channeling activities, i.e. supervising as a messenger, tutor, helper

Modifying behavior by
- assigning the child to "cooling corner" for a set time and saying, "You may not stay with people if you act like a bully. I won't let you hurt people and they may not hurt you, either."
- using a response - cost system
- letting the child show off something they can do well

How Am I Going To Respond?

Strokes / Rewards

Leisure

Fun & Humor

Letting Go

Limit Setting

Time Management

Prioritize Choices

Realign Expectations

Chapter 16
● ● ● ● ● ● ● ● ● ● ● ● ●

MANAGING OUR STRESS

Have you ever had one of those days? If you are honest you might have one of those days every week, every day, even every hour! So, imagine that the families we work with are in the same situation. They may even be more stressed than we can understand... financially, medically, or just tired, lonely, or overwhelmed. Children are great imitators and can feel stress before we even recognize it in ourselves. They also show signs differently than adults seem to show them. This chapter is geared toward letting us sit back and measure the amount and type of stress we find ourselves in daily! Feel free to explore the causes and solutions that are included. Parents may need to seek help from others when they are at the "end of their rope"... now you can offer a hand!

Faculty Handouts

Faculty Activity

● ●

Stress Management

A lecturer, when explaining stress management to an audience, raised a glass of water and asked, "How heavy is this glass of water?" Answers called out ranged from 20g to 500g. The lecturer replied, "The absolute weight doesn't matter. It depends on how long you try to hold it. If I hold it for a minute, that's not a problem. If I hold it for an hour, I'll have an ache in my right arm. If I hold it for a day, you'll have to call an ambulance. In each case, it's the same weight, but the longer I hold it, the heavier it becomes." He continued, "And that's the way it is with stress management. If we carry our burdens all the time, sooner or later, as the burden becomes increasingly heavy, we won't be able to carry on. As with the glass of water, you have to put it down for a while and rest before holding it again. When we're refreshed, we can carry on with the burden. So, before you return home tonight, put the burden of work down. Don't carry it home. You can pick it up tomorrow. Whatever burdens you're carrying now, let them down for a moment if you can." So, my friend, why not take a while to just simply RELAX. Put down anything that may be a burden to you right now. Don't pick it up again until after you've rested a while. Life is short.

- Source Unknown

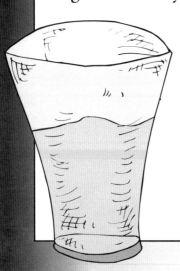

STRESS RELIEVER

Purpose: This is a great icebreaker before the beginning of a faculty meeting or in-service to relieve stress and demonstrate creativity.

Materials: Paper, pencils, poster board

Procedures: Write the following phrases on your poster board:

To dress the turkey	To break a leg
To fly off the handle	To fall to pieces
To take the cake	To rain cats and dogs
To pick up the house	To die laughing
To hold your tongue	To scream your head off

Other:_____

Hold up the poster with the phrases written on it. Ask the participants to spend five minutes being creative. Have them draw their favorite ones... (abstracts allowed) and take a minute or two to share the results. Some people say that they can't draw and this is a great time to explain that we are not looking for perfection... just fun and creativity!

Recognizing Signs of Stress

- ❑ Anger
- ❑ Anxiety
- ❑ Clumsiness
- ❑ Constant Error in Judgement
- ❑ Diarrhea
- ❑ Feeling Powerless
- ❑ Feeling of Being "Uptight"
- ❑ Forgetfulness
- ❑ Headaches
- ❑ Inability to Make Decisions

- ❑ Indigestion
- ❑ Irritability
- ❑ Knotted Stomach
- ❑ Lack of Energy
- ❑ Loss of Hope
- ❑ Overeating or Skipping Meals
- ❑ Sadness or Lack of Interest
- ❑ Sleep Disturbances

What is Stress?

Not surprisingly … everybody experiences stress. It is the body's natural reaction to tension, pressure, and change. Can you believe that a certain amount of stress helps to make life more challenging and less boring? I know, as an educator, you can do without the extra challenges some days!

Actually, too much stress can be bad for you in several different ways. Physically you may experience many REAL health symptoms which may result in a visit to your healthcare provider. Mentally it can play havoc with your emotions and can affect your relationships with others. If you have prolonged unresolved stress, however, it can lead to accidental injury or even serious illness.

For your sake and the others in your life, it is important for you to recognize and manage stress before it gets the best of you and compromises your health and safety!

Ways to Manage Stress

1. Surround yourself with those people who value positive thinking.

2. Don't think that you are the only one that can do something! Ask for help if tasks are too big for you alone!

3. Learn flexibility and know you can not control all situations.

4. Lists, lists, lists are a great aide to assist you to break down the tasks that you face every day or week!

5. Eat well balanced meals ... don't skip them & limit pure sugars.

6. Get plenty of sleep at night.

7. Moderate exercise each day boosts your energy level and can improve your mood as it assists with blood pressure, blood sugars, cholesterol, and stamina.

8. Make time to do the things you enjoy. Relax, listen to music, read, play with pets, and generally have some FUN!

9. Think of mistakes as new opportunities to learn.

10. Laugh! Look for the humor in situations that relate to you or others in your life.

Teachers' Relaxation Method
Take 5 minutes of your planning period

We all have that extra bit of tension sometimes that finds it's way into various parts of our bodies. You will be amazed at the quick energy and relief you will gain if you set aside a few minutes for yourself! We can also train our students to do the following muscle tension & release techniques to help them let go of built-up stress before tests! Follow the steps and you'll feel refreshed in no time!

Sit on a chair with both feet flat on the ground. It is nice to have harsh lights off to limit distraction. It helps to learn these steps so you don't have to read them.

1. **RIGHT HAND & FOREARM** : make a tight fist : release it

2. **RIGHT UPPER ARM** : bend arm and make a strong "muscle" : let down arm

3. **LEFT HAND & FOREARM** : make a tight fist : release it

4. **LEFT UPPER ARM** : bend arm and make a strong "muscle" : let down arm

5. **FOREHEAD** : raise eyebrows up : relax your face

6. **EYES & CHEEKS** : squeeze eyes shut : relax

7. **MOUTH & JAW** : clench your teeth & pull your lips back : release

8. **NECK** : lock hands behind your head & push your head back against your hands but the head doesn't really move : relax

9. **SHOULDERS & BACK** : take a deep breath & pull your arms & shoulders back : let your shoulders hang from your arms at your side

10. **STOMACH** : pull in and tighten : release

11. **CALVES** : raise up the heels : put feet flat

12. **FEET** : crunch up your toes : relax

Chapter 17

•••••••••••••

LOOKING FOR IMPERFECTIONS...
Something to Laugh About!

Being human offers us many opportunities to see the limitations that we each display daily. This chapter focuses on our weaknesses and not our strengths. It is important to find the humor in our shortcomings! Children often view grown-ups as being able to do everything better than they can. It must be that we just correct our "goofs" quietly and go on about our business. We certainly make our fair share of mistakes. When was the last time you dialed the wrong number, forgot to call the pharmacy, locked your keys in the car, or arrived at the grocery checkout line without checks in your checkbook? It has happened to the best of us... join the crowd! In this chapter, you will be challenged to learn to read all over again ... for the first time! Good luck! Maybe this activity will help remind you that at times, school can be a frustrating experience from the eyes of a child.

Faculty Activities

Faculty Handouts

IS 99.9% GOOD ENOUGH?

⇨ Two million documents will be lost by the IRS this year.

⇨ 22,000 checks will be deducted from the wrong bank accounts in the next 60 minutes.

⇨ Twelve babies will be given to the wrong parents each day.

⇨ Two planes at O'Hare International in Chicago will be unsafe.

⇨ 291 pacemaker operations will be performed incorrectly this year.

- Source Unknown

YOUR FIRST READER

Purpose: This activity points out the fact that even intelligent adults sometimes find it difficult to learn new things at a rapid pace! It will remind faculty members of what a frustrating experience school can be for children.

Materials: Copy of this booklet, overhead (optional)

Procedures: This book uses only 14 words. It can be used as a flip book; but it is best used on the overhead to control the speed of presenting each page to the group. Each word is used several times, since repetition helps in learning to read. Only one or two words are introduced on a page. Have the participants read straight through this story without looking back!

After allowing participants to get slightly confused and maybe a little frustrated, review the Story Key on page 113 and discuss the frustration involved in learning something completely new at a very fast pace.

(SAM)

1

👎👎✡️

DDY)

2

☹️🏳️🏳️😐
(LOOK)

👎✌️👎👎✡️,

☹️🏳️🏳️😐, ☹️🏳️🏳️😐.

3

 ,

(AT)   (ME)

4

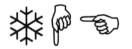
(THE)   (DOG)

5

(SEE)

(JUMP)

6

(DON'T)

(HIM)

7

(CAN)

(TOO)

Your First Reader - Story Key

Page 1   Sam

Page 2   Daddy

Page 3   Look Daddy, look, look.

Page 4   Look Daddy. Look at me.

Page 5   Look Daddy, look at the dog.

Page 6   See me Daddy. See me jump. See me jump at the dog.

Page 7   Don't jump at the dog, Sam. Don't jump at him. Look at the dog Sam.

Page 8   Daddy, the dog can jump at me. Jump, dog, jump! See me jump, dog!

Page 9   Daddy can see Sam jump, too! Sam can jump, jump, jump!

Time To Share

Spend this time reflecting on a situation that was a "Super" mistake in your life.
Share in your writing what you learned as a lesson from this experience.

This is a true story of my biggest GOOF!

Chapter 18

● ● ● ● ● ● ● ● ● ● ● ●

BULLYING

I remember watching the Learning Channel on television and sitting in awe as I watched one of the first victims of bullying... the caveman!!! One of the big guys clubs the weaker one and takes his dinner from him. Sounds like a tale from school where the bully steals the little kid's lunch money, right? It has been happening as long as we can remember, but today we see it escalating to more dangerous and harmful consequences! The ridicule and name-calling are becoming more than can be tolerated. We see the results with the tragic shootings in our schools over the past several years. Our students are not recognizing the need to band together to voice disapproval of the bullies' actions. It is time to stand up for each other and show that being bullied will not be accepted in our schools!

Student Activities

Student Handout

Parent Handout

THIS IS ME!

Purpose: This activity teaches children to respect each other and each others' choices.

Materials: Construction paper, markers / crayons

Procedures: On a piece of construction paper have the students write their name (you can join in and do your own) in big letters across the middle of the page any way they choose. After they do this, give them the following instructions:

Right Top Corner: Write down or illustrate something you enjoy doing with your peers.

Left Top Corner: Write down or illustrate something that you are good at that others might not expect.

Right Bottom Corner: Write down or illustrate something you have done that you are proud of.

Left Bottom Corner: Write down or illustrate something that you have done that you regretted afterwards.

Have the students stand up and share their name plate with the class. Instruct the class that students can ask questions but laughing and negative words are off limits. After they have all shared explain to the class that everyone likes and enjoys different things and that is what makes us unique. Remind them by telling them, "We shouldn't judge our peers by what they like and do not like. Getting to know someone that may not do the same things or like the exact things you like is an opportunity for you to grow and learn something. We should all respect each others' choices."

BULLYING 101

Bullying is when someone continually harasses you by threatening, name calling, excluding you from activities, physically hurting you or destroying/stealing your property, or making you feel uncomfortable or afraid you are being bullied. Both boys and girls bully.

Bullying is NOT O. K . - EVER. It is not just playing or clowning around. It is very serious. After incidents like Columbine, schools are taking major measures to stop students from bullying and protect the ones that are or have been bullied.

People who are bullied are often different from others. This might be something physical like wearing glasses, being shorter or taller than others, or having braces. They may not be good at physical activities like running or football or be extremely intelligent or have trouble academically in school. Others might be bullied because of their race or religion. People who are bullied are often thought to not be able to stand up for themselves thus are easy targets.

Bullies bully because they like to act tough and want the attention. They are usually the ones people are drawn to because they are often outspoken and appear "tough." Most have a false sense of self esteem where they feel superior to others. They want control of others because in reality most times they have no control in their own lives. They may have been bullied themselves in the past.

If you are being bullied, NEVER fight the bully. This will only make things worse. If walking away and firmly telling him/ her to STOP does not work you must tell someone. Hang out with friends and not alone. Bullies pick on ones who are always by themselves.

Some kids are afraid to tell because the bully has threatened them. You are giving him/ her the power if you don't tell. No one deserves to be bullied. Telling an adult you trust will make you feel better and help you in getting the situation resolved. ALWAYS TELL AN ADULT!!!!! DON'T WAIT.

Here are some things you want to remember when dealing with a bully: DON'T KEEP IT A SECRET. Remember, no one deserves to be bullied. If you try and deal with it on your own and it doesn't work the FIRST time, don't continue to try. TELL SOMEONE YOU TRUST. If you don't tell, the bully has that much more power over you. DON'T HIT OR TRY TO FIGHT THE BULLY. You will end up in trouble just like the bully. Some people fight when they can't stand it any longer. Don't let it get that far.

LAST --- Everyone is entitled to live their life and do things they want to do. Walk with your head held high. Be proud of who you are. Look people in the eye when you are walking and send a message that you are a confident human being!!

TIPS FOR PARENTS ABOUT BULLYING

How To Tell If Your Child Might Be A Victim of Bullying

- He / She just weeks ago looked forward to going to school and couldn't wait to share the days events. However, lately the child does not seem interested and does not offer any news about the day. When asked, he / she shrugs it off as "nothing special happened."

- Your child suddenly does not feel well every morning before school to the point of tears.

- He / She is having trouble sleeping. The child either comes home from school only wanting to go to sleep or at night has trouble going to sleep.

- Your child is suddenly failing or his / her grades are dropping.

- He / She seems isolated and sad all the time.

- Your child has come home several times without a backpack or has reported "losing" his / her lunch money or other belongings.

What Do You Do Now?

- Don't wait. Talk to your child. Some parents think that kids will work things out. If your child is being bullied chances are he / she is crying for help and you just don't know it. Sit down and talk to your child. Listen and assure him / her that it is not his / her fault.

- The way you react plays a HUGE part with how your child is going to feel now that it is out in the open. You may be upset or even angry but do not show it. Your child might think you are mad at him/ her or even disappointed. This is your time to be supportive.

- It is typical for children to develop low self-esteem when being bullied. Tell your child that they should feel proud and brave that he/ she has chosen to come forward and that you know that must be scary. You can tell him/ her you are proud of them but your goal is to have the child feel it for him/ herself.

- Make a plan together. Bullying should not be tolerated by any means at school. Call your school counselor first and talk to him/ her and your child's teacher to let them know what is going on.

- It's important that you let your child know that fighting back is not the answer. Encourage your child to always have a buddy with them and steer clear of the bully until the school can get involved.

WE ALL SHINE BRIGHT

Purpose: This activity demonstrates to participants that they can all use their individual strengths and talents to work together and accomplish great things!

Materials: Glow bracelets / necklaces (one for each student)

Procedures: Hand out a glow bracelet / necklace to each participant and dim the lights in the room. Tell them not do anything with the bracelet until instructed. As you are handing out the bracelets / necklaces have the participants imagine that the bracelets represent the group and each individual in it.

After they have all been distributed, tell them to carefully snap the bracelet / necklace just once until they see a small glimmer of light and then STOP. Say, "That one little glow represents you. What do you bring to the group? What is something that you contribute?" Instruct them to snap it again. Tell them that snap represents a peer. "What is something that you might not be necessarily good at that someone else might be?"

Have participants continue to snap the bracelet in different spots and with each snap explain that additional bit of light is one more person. As they continue to snap the bracelet, encourage them to think about each other's strengths and talents. Encourage them to notice that with each snap the bracelet glows a little bit more. Now, instruct them to stop. Have them share what they see. They will notice that although they snap it in many places the entire bracelet is still not glowing.

Have participants shake the bracelet. They will see, as they shake it, the glow of the bracelet becomes one as the glowing blends. When we work together as a unit, as a family, things fall into place. Without shaking the bracelet, the parts of the bracelet that were glowing were not united. But putting it together made it become one. As a family, a group, and / or a class we all have to work together and do our part. In closing, encourage the participants to look at their bracelets glowing and think about the fact that "their one glow" did not make the whole thing light up. It was about each snap, each person. Sometimes things are not just about "us." It is about everyone. Whether you are shy or outgoing, athletic or a scholar everyone has a part and something to contribute. Together we become one.

Have each person then place their bracelet on someone else to show that we are in this together and we don't all have to be alike to accomplish something productive and successful.

Chapter 19

• • • • • • • • • • • • •

KEEPING UP WITH THE HYPERACTIVE CHILD

Do you have energy to spare? Probably not if you've spent the day keeping up with "Johnny Jump-up!" Often these bright, clumsy, well-intentioned, impulsive, or forgetful children take time and effort to attend to their needs. Although it can prove to be a challenge to attend to the hyperative children's needs as well as the needs of the other children in your class, it is also a great opportunity to meet some incredible risk-takers and inventors. These children may have no sense of time but they can usually figure out a quicker way to travel from point A to point B. The following chapter includes ideas that are aimed to make learning a positive experience for the hyperactive child and the others in the class as well!

Student Activity

Faculty Handouts

STAYING ON TASK

Purpose: This brainstorming activity helps children think about what gets them into trouble and also what they can do to stay out of trouble.

Materials: Chart paper, marker

Procedures: Brainstorm with the class situations that often get them into trouble. Some examples might be talking at inappropriate times, being up out of seat, being off task, etc. Write examples down on a piece of chart paper. After everyone has had a chance to share, tell the students that now you want them to think of ways to PREVENT these things from happening. As the brainstorming is taking place feel free to suggest situations that you know are hard for some students and also ways to prevent the behavior. Next, have the students get in pairs and have them illustrate each situation and the prevention. The next day have each pair share their completed work with the class. Display on the wall low enough for students to see. For this to work it is important that you refer to the wall often, especially for the students who have a hard time staying on task. Seeing the situations and preventions will help keep the students focused on good behavior.

EXAMPLES OF BRAINSTORMING ACTIVITY

Situations that might keep us from being on task and learning:

* Talking when teacher is talking
* Being up out of seat
* Shouting out
* Going through desk instead of listening
* Playing with objects on desk
* Talking to neighbor

Things we can do to prevent us from being off task:

* Sit still in desk.
* Pay attention to teacher at all times.
* Stop and think before speaking.
* Clear off desk when teacher is explaining a lesson.
* Sit near teacher and / or away from people you might talk to.

TIPS WHEN WORKING WITH THE HYPERACTIVE CHILD

Assignments

Children who are hyperactive do not stay focused for long. You have to engage them in small activities. Don't give them something and expect them to complete it independently within a class period (30-45 minutes). Break up the assignment into small parts and have the child check in with you when that part is complete.

Visuals

Having a schedule posted on the child's desk is a great tool. If the student knows what is coming up it helps him/ her stay focused on the task at hand. *Remember:* The hyperactive brain is 10 steps ahead of ours!

It will help if you or the child can make a list of things they have to do for the day. Now remember, if you let the child make the list, you might need to look at it first!!

Using a timer for the student is also helpful. You can give the child a certain amount of time to complete a certain number of problems or whatever task he/ she is being given.

Buddy/ Peer Helper

Having a buddy serve as a peer helper for the child can be extremely useful. You want to pick someone that the child can relate to but cannot manipulate. The peer helper is there to model good organization, as well as good behavior. Make sure you follow up with the helper periodically to see how things are going. You don't want to have the helper become too overwhelmed!

Words of Encouragement

All children respond positively to encouragement. If a child knows that you are there and care he/ she will move mountains to please. Use encouraging words like, "Look how far you are!" or "You are really working hard!," or "Wow, look at that." All of these put the responsibility on the student and in turn makes the student work harder. As long as the tasks are small and can be completed in a fairly short amount of time, the hyperactive child most likely will not have a problem completing the task.

Work Space

Trying to have any student sit for a long period of time to complete an assignment is challenge enough. Add a dose of hyperactivity and it becomes a major power struggle. If a child works better on the floor, in the corner, or even under his/ her desk, consider giving him/ her that freedom. If children do not abuse the privilege and that is what it is, then it fosters independence. It would be more enjoyable to sit on a bean bag to practice multiplication, than at a desk!!

ADHD STATISTICS

Attention Deficit Hyperactive Disorder is a developmental disorder describing distractibility, difficulties with controlled behavior, focusing, hyperactivity, and restlessness.

• Almost 3-7% of the US population have ADHD. (Barkley, 2006)

• Symptoms of ADHD often begin between the ages of 3 and 6. (Barkley, 2006)

• Boys are more likely to have ADHD than girls, with a 3:1 ratio. (Barkley, 2006)

• Over 50% of children with ADHD have a greater risk of developing oppositional and defiant behavior. (Barkley, 2006)

• 25% often have self-esteem issues and problems with depression. (Barkley, 2006)

• Nearly 30% of ADHD children have a learning disability in reading, writing, or math. (ICSI, 2005)

• Over 50% of children with ADHD have communication difficulties that become social skills deficits. (ICSI, 2005)

• Teenagers with ADHD, within their first 2-5 years of driving have nearly four times more accidents and have three times as many citations for speeding than teenage drivers without ADHD. (Barkley, 2006)

• 30-50% have failed or repeated a year of school. (Barkley, 2006)

• Nearly 40% never graduate high school. (Barkley, 2006)

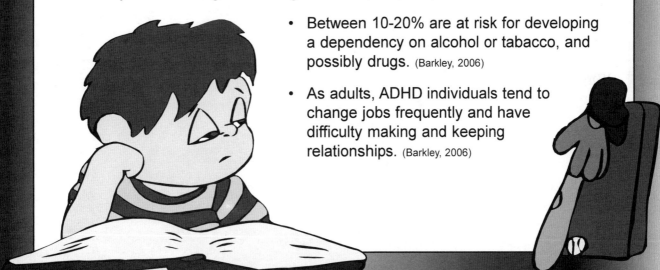

• Between 10-20% are at risk for developing a dependency on alcohol or tabacco, and possibly drugs. (Barkley, 2006)

• As adults, ADHD individuals tend to change jobs frequently and have difficulty making and keeping relationships. (Barkley, 2006)

Chapter 20

REMINDER CUES FOR EVERYDAY

Share these posters with parents to assist with the nagging tasks of daily living skills! They can be placed in prominent places where a child might need reminders... front door at home, refrigerator, bedroom, etc. The students are visually prompted to complete certain jobs that are necessary for proper hygiene and organization. It is a non-threatening way to use non-verbal reminders that are necessary for children as they grow!

Parent / Student Handouts

MORNING REMINDERS

MAKE YOUR BED

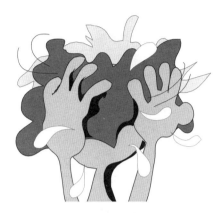

WASH UP

COMB/ BRUSH HAIR

BRUSH TEETH

DRESS

EAT BREAKFAST

GETTING TO SCHOOL REMINDERS

GET BACKPACK

LUNCH & HOMEWORK

BOOKS & GLASSES

SIGNED PAPERS

SCHOOL SUPPLIES

READY TO LEARN

EVENING REMINDERS

HEALTHY AFTER-SCHOOL SNACK

WELL-LIT PLACE TO WORK

GET SOME EXERCISE

DO YOUR CHORES

GET ENOUGH SLEEP

PLAY A GAME, READ, & RELAX

HOW TO KEEP PEOPLE CLOSE

DRAW A PICTURE FOR THEM

HOLD SOMETHING SPECIAL OF THEIRS

WRITE THEM A LETTER

HELP WITH IMPORTANT PROJECTS

SPEND TIME TOGETHER

CALL ON THE PHONE

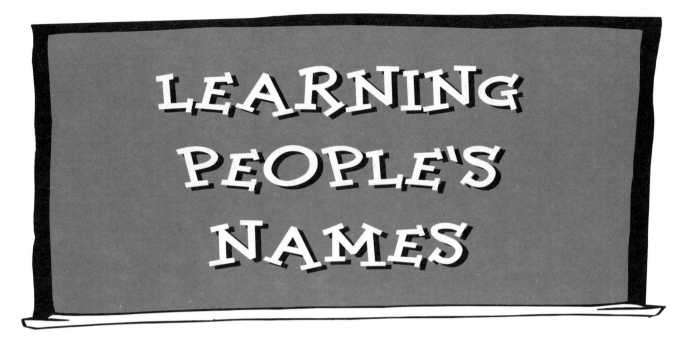

Chapter 21

LEARNING PEOPLE'S NAMES

This chapter offers techniques to give a touch of variety to learning the names of students, peers, parents and other groups of people. It is very impressive to master the art of calling others by their name. People feel important when someone takes the time and effort to remember to call them by their given names. They know that you have paid attention to an important detail that identifies them as an individual. The following ideas are pretty straight-forward and some of them make learning names into a game! Whatever it takes, the results will be appreciated by everyone!

Faculty / Student Activities

THE NAME CARD

Purpose: This activity gives group members the opportunity to meet someone new and introduce them to the rest of the room.

Materials: 5" x 7" index cards, markers

Procedures: Each peson in the group has a 5" x 7" index card and markers available on each table where they will be seated. They are invited to meet someone in the room that they are not familiar with and spend five minutes getting to know some interesting fact that no one else in the room knows. Their partner gets another five minutes to find out an interesting fact, too. Everyone returns to their seats and creates a unique name card for their partner that includes a hint or drawing that they can share with the larger group. It is fun to see if the other group members can guess the fact by seeing the name card!!!

ALPHABET LINE-UP

Purpose: This activity is great for the visual learners in the group to associate names and faces with positions in a line.

Procedures: Invite the participants to arrange themselves in alphabetical order by their first names. This task forces participants to find out other names in the group.

Option: As a twist, do a "nonverbal name line-up" as a way to review names after participants have introduced themselves in the conventional fashion. Ask them to line up in order *without talking to each other!*

NAME TAG MIX-UP

Purpose: This activity gives group members the opportunity to mingle and learn many new names before finding the owner of the name tag they were assigned.

Materials: Name tags

Procedures: Give each person the name tag of someone else in the group and ask that they each find the owner of the tag they have in their possession. Invite the people to circulate until each person has received his or her own name tag!

> ## My name is:

DO YOU KNOW ME?

Purpose: This activity is a fun way to learn the names of everyone in a group.

Procedures: Form a circle and place one person in the center. Ask that person to point to someone in the circle and challenge him or her with the question ... " Do you know your neighbors?" If the person in the circle can successfully say the name of the people immediately to his / her right and left, the person in the middle stays there and challenges another person in the circle. When the participant fails the neighbor test, they replace the person in the middle. As the game goes on, frequently change positions of the participants.

WHO IS IT?

Purpose: This activity gives group members the opportunity to introduce themselves to the group and also recollect the names of others.

Material: Beanbag or ball

Procedures: Have group members stand in a circle with one person holding an object that can be easily thrown and caught, such as a beanbag or ball. The member holding the object says his or her name and tosses the object to another group member. The person catching it gives his or her name and tosses to another member. Continue until everyone has stated their name. When the final member has been introduced, ask the person with the object to now toss it to a person after calling their name. The receiver then repeats the name of the person that threw it and says the name of the other group member before tossing the object to them.

WHAT'S IN A NAME?

Purpose: This activity gives group members the opportunity to share a little more about themselves than just their name. This added information helps others to recall their name later.

Procedures: Have participants introduce themselves and then share any of the following about their names:

- What they like or dislike about their name.

- Who they were named after.

- A nickname that they like or dislike & who gave it to them.

- The origin of their name.

- What they've always wished they were called.

Chapter 22

ETHICS IN SCHOOLS

In a staff meeting, the topic of confidentiality and ethical behavior can bring about a lively conversation. It is so easy for even "seasoned" teachers to forget that we are always set up to be models of professionalism. Sometimes without even realizing what we are saying we carry on conversations in public places that should only happen behind closed doors with those that need to be involved. Conversations such as, "Have you heard about the child that everyone knows... who was sent to the Alternative Center for bringing a... and his mother couldn't be reached at... and the resource officer went to the house and..." may be typical of something you may overhear in the front office. The only people needed in this loop would include the classroom teacher, counselor and administrator. However, others that may have caught wind of this conversation could have been the nurse in the office, the secretary, the mom that was enrolling her child, the next door neighbor dropping off lunch, and the grade level teammates! This is a devastating situation for the child involved in the situation! This chapter explores ways to deal with the issues of confidentiality and ethics in schools.

Faculty Handouts

ETHICAL REMINDERS

It is always wise to look back at your past choices. Being human gives us the opportunity to continually learn from our MISTAKES!

1. Relationships

- Superiors
- Co-Workers
- Parents
- Students

2. Record Keeping

- Watch Loose Info on Desks
- Computer Screens & E-mail
- Written Documents & Phone Logs

3. Confidentiality Awareness

- Who
- What
- Where
- Need to Know ONLY

4. Reporting Abuse

5. Use Caution in Front Office, Halls & Lounge!

> **REMEMBER:**
> In the community, you are still an educator!

THINK ABOUT THIS...

As professionals, we have an obligation to protect the privacy of all students and should not disclose confidential information without expressed written consent, except where permitted by the law.

It is also of utmost concern that we respect each individual and guard against discrimination based on the following: gender, race, religion, age, national origin, disability, sexual orientation, or economic conditions.

A confusing issue stems from the ethics involved in social relationships with our students and their families. Where is the fineline that can be crossed in these matters?

Remember to always ...

- ❖ Stop
- ❖ Look
- ❖ Listen
- ❖ Think before you act
- ❖ If in doubt, always ASK!

CONFIDENTIALITY

Gossip vs. Professional Sharing of Information

When talking to a colleague about a student or his family, apply these simple tests to see if the discussion may be violating the rights of the student.

1. What is discussed

a. If it involves personally identifiable information that is confidential (such as; handicapping condition, family data, etc.) the parties should be sure that legitimate educational interest is involved.

b. If the discussion involves information that is unsubstantiated rumor, subjective opinion, or hearsay, chances are that confidentiality will be in question, and the parties have moved from professionalism to gossip.

2. Where the discussion takes place

a. In a private place such as a teacher's empty room, a counselor's office, or the teacher's lounge when it is empty, there should be no problem.

b. If it occurs in a public place such as the playground, the halls, teacher's lunch room or supermarket aisle, there is a very good chance that confidentiality will be violated.

3. Who is listening

a. If the parties are school officials with a legitimate educational interest in the child, there is no problem.

b. If others that are listening have no legitimate educational interest, such as an eavesdropping teacher, a nosy child on the playground or kids in line in the hall, confidentiality may be violated.

4. Why the discussion took place

a. If the parties are sharing info that will help them work with the student there is no problem

b. If the parties are gossiping to pass time, for non-educational reasons, or to carry tales about the family there is a problem with confidentiality.

Appendix
●●●●●●●●●●●●●

APPENDIX
of CERTIFICATES
and POSTERS

Certificates

Posters

Certificate of Appreciation

For all of your extra time!

Awarded To: _____

_____
Authorized Signature

Date: _____

You are a key to

Student Success

This Certificate is Awarded to:

_____

Date

_____

Authorized Signature

You are most Helpful!

This certificate is awarded to

Authorized by:

Date of award:

Super Great Job

Been "kneading" to tell you

This Certificate is Awarded to:

Authorized Signature

Date of Signature

Certificate for Over and Above the Call of Duty

Out of this World

This Certificate is Awarded to:

_____

Authorized Signature

Date:

I'm a FAN of yours!

Date: _____

Thanks for being refreshing

This Certificate is Awarded to:

_____

Authorized Signature

Attitude +

Ambition =

Achievement

Children are our Future!!!

We are PROUD to work in EDUCATION

Together We Can

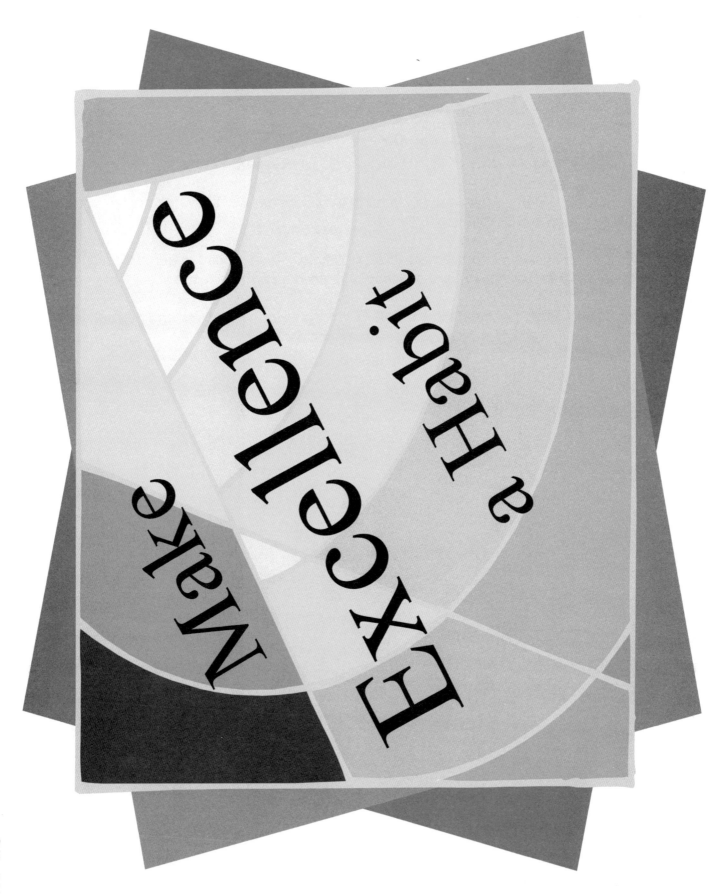

Make Excellence a Habit.

References

Barkley, R. (2006). *About ADHD - A fact sheet.* (on-line), Available: http://www.russellbarkley.org/adhd-facts.htm

Barkley, R. (2001). *Taking charge of ADHD.* New York: The Guilford Press.

Bowman & Bowman (1997). *Meaningful Mentoring: A handbook of effective strategies, projects and activities.* Chapin, SC: YouthLight, Inc.

Institute for Clinical Systems Improvement (2005). *Diagnosis and management of attention deficit hyperactivity disorder in primary care of school age children and adolescents.*

Institute for Clinical Systems Improvement (1997). *Recognizing child abuse and neglect.* Bloomington, MN. Available: http://www.new-life.net/chldsaf4.htm